"Inspiring, challenging, propelling. This book reminds us that God accomplishes the extraordinary through the ordinary. Gregg Matte's *Unstoppable Gospel* is a brilliant reminder that we are all invited into a story much bigger than we could ever imagine."

—**Louie Giglio**, Passion City Church/Passion Conferences

"What I've always admired and appreciated about Gregg is his ability to communicate with profound wisdom and everyday practicality at the same time. His new book, *Unstoppable Gospel*, is no exception. To me, this book echoes Paul's words in Colossians: 'the mystery is revealed, Christ in you, the hope of glory.' The gospel is the profound and the practical wrapped together in you and me as followers of Jesus. I am grateful to recommend this good work of writing to all of you."

—**Chris Tomlin**, Dove Award–winning worship leader
and songwriter

"God has used Gregg Matte to challenge me in my faith for over twenty years now. Gregg is a dynamic storyteller and gifted at making the Bible come alive in a real, applicable way. In his new book, *Unstoppable Gospel*, that's exactly what he does as he tells the story of the original church and how God used a few people to change the world forever through the power of the Holy Spirit. If you're looking for a book that will challenge you, inspire you, and equip you to change your community, nation, and the world for Jesus, then open up the pages of *Unstoppable Gospel* and start reading. You won't regret a minute of it!"

—**Melanie Shankle**, *New York Times* bestselling author
of *Sparkly Green Earrings*

"*Unstoppable Gospel* calls all Christ-followers to rise in our generation to risk it all and change the world! This is the message that the church desperately needs. It is past time to stop playing it safe! Gregg Matte calls us to live out this unstoppable gospel boldly, and then we will see this unstoppable kingdom of God advance exponentially."

—**Dr. Ronnie Floyd**, president, Southern Baptist Convention;
senior pastor, Cross Church

UNSTOPPABLE
GOSPEL

Living Out the World-Changing Vision

of Jesus's First Followers

GREGG MATTE

BakerBooks

a division of Baker Publishing Group

Grand Rapids, Michigan

© 2015 by Gregg Matte

Published by Baker Books
a division of Baker Publishing Group
P.O. Box 6287, Grand Rapids, MI 49516-6287
www.bakerbooks.com

Printed in the United States of America

Library of Congress Cataloging-in-Publication Data
Matte, Gregg.
    Unstoppable gospel : living out the world-changing vision of Jesus's first
followers / Gregg Matte.
        pages cm
    Includes bibliographical references.
    ISBN 978-0-8010-0635-7 (pbk.)
    1. Bible. Acts—Criticism, interpretation, etc. 2. First Baptist Church
(Houston, Tex.) I. Title.
BS2625.52.M377 2015
226.6′06—dc23   2015020253

Scripture quotations are from the Holman Christian Standard Bible, copyright 1999, 2000, 2002, 2003, 2009 by Holman Bible Publishers. Used by permission.

15 16 17 18 19 20 21   7 6 5 4 3 2 1

This book is dedicated to the people of Houston's First Baptist Church. The book of Acts and Mission 1:8 has changed us forever. This is our story, our journey with God. What a ride! It's hard to believe God has even more for us. I'm privileged and honored to be your pastor.

Contents

Acknowledgments

I have learned through the years that I'm a speaker who writes, not a writer who speaks. Both are needed, but as a friend once told me, "You have to find your lane." So there are many people I would like to thank for their contribution to *Unstoppable Gospel*.

My research team volunteers at Houston's First Baptist Church: your prayer, wisdom, and depth are a blessing. My fellow Houston's First staff and church members: without your hard work Mission 1:8 and countless other ministries would still be only ideas. It is an honor to serve with you.

My editor, Jim Denney: I'm grateful for your work and skill. My literary agent, Don Gates: your expertise has opened new doors for me. Lifeway: for producing the accompanying study guide. My publisher, Baker Books: I'm glad to be on your team. Thank you for all you have done to make this book a reality.

My family and friends who have been such an encouragement: you are a shaping influence in my life.

Greyson and Valerie: I'm so proud to be your dad. Great days are ahead of you and I pray you live these pages.

My wife, Kelly: words are too few to describe my love for you. No one on Planet Earth has supported and listened to me more on this book. I'm grateful to have you as my wife and best friend.

Most of all I'm thankful to Jesus, who knows me better and loves me more than anyone. I'm so amazed at how He has blessed me and is using me.

Introduction

In April 2012, the cover of *Newsweek* magazine depicted Jesus dressed in a denim jacket, plaid shirt, and a crown of thorns, standing on a Manhattan street. The headline read, "Forget the Church. Follow Jesus."[1]

Forget the church? We hear this refrain all the time these days. Some people ask, "Can't I just be spiritual? Can't I have Jesus without going to church?"

It's easy to understand why many are frustrated with the church. We see divided churches where Christians can't get along. We see churches that are little more than theological debating societies that have no impact on the world around them. And there's that time-honored gripe, "The church is full of hypocrites."

Are there hypocrites in the church? Sure. A few, but not as many as some people think. Hypocrites, after all, are people who pretend to be something they're not. From where I sit, there aren't all that many hypocrites in the church. I think the problem is that when people say "hypocrites," they really mean "sinners." And yes, the church is loaded with people struggling with sin.

But that doesn't mean we're all hypocrites. It simply means we're all *human*, and we're struggling to become more and more like Christ. As someone once said, "If you find the perfect church, don't join it—you'll ruin it."

If you've ever read 1 and 2 Corinthians, you know that all the ills of the church today were commonplace in the first-century church in Corinth: divisiveness, immorality, backstabbing, and more. From New Testament times the church has been plagued by the sins, pettiness, and failings of its people. The church has long had an image problem, and there have always been those willing to write the church off as a failed institution.

Even some Christians want us to forget the church. But Jesus has not left that option open to us. He has made no provision for us to follow Him while living in isolation from other believers. Instead, He tells us, "On this rock I will build My church, and the forces of Hades will not overpower it" (Matt. 16:18). This comes on the heels of Jesus asking, "Who do you say I am?"

He confirmed His deity and then the vehicle by which He would become known on earth in perpetuity: the church. And before He went to the cross, Jesus prayed that we Christians would live together in love (see John 14–17).

We know that "Christ loved the church and gave Himself for her to make her holy" (Eph. 5:25–26). We're also told that the church has an exalted mission before it: "This is so God's multi-faceted wisdom may now be made known through the church to the rulers and authorities in the heavens" (3:10). God has put into motion an unstoppable force—the church. There is nothing like it as a force for good in society.

For all its flaws and failings, the church demonstrates the wisdom of God. And that's why Satan hates the church, and continually tries to destroy, discredit, and defeat it. So if you hate the church, you need to ask yourself whose side you're really on. If you're on God's side, if you want to be used by God to demonstrate His wisdom to "the rulers and authorities in the heavens," then you need to learn to love His church.

Jesus loved it—and so should we. His message to us is, "Love Me, love My church. I gave Myself up for it, so how can you love Me while hating My church?"

In my own life, if you hate my bride, Kelly, then I have to assume that you don't like me much either.

The Lord loves the church, empowers the church, and uses the church to accomplish His purposes. The church is His chosen means of reaching the lost with the Good News of salvation. The church is His vehicle for loving the poor, the sick, the prisoners, the widows, and the orphans.

The biggest difference maker in the heavens and in society is not to be relegated to singing pretty songs once a week; it is to be unleashed as the people of God scatter to neighborhoods and office desks and classrooms. As believers, *we are the church*. If we want to revive it, that begins with reviving ourselves. God's purpose is for the church to be more than just an event on Sunday morning; it's meant to be a fuse lit to unleash the explosive power of a believer's life.

Do we in the church often seem like a bunch of squabbling, selfish sinners? Absolutely! The church that bears the name of Jesus often fails to demonstrate His character. Yet Jesus will not let us go. In spite of all our flaws and failings, Jesus loves the church—and so should we.

Jesus designed the church to be a laboratory of love, where we learn through experience and experiment to give and receive grace, mercy, and forgiveness. The church is where we learn what it truly means to love one another. Jesus has not given up on us, in spite of our failings. His plea to us is: "Don't give up on My church."

So come with me on a journey through the exciting early days—*and* present days—of the church. We'll rediscover what made the early church so powerful—and *unstoppable*. We'll see the book of Acts open with a room full of huddled, scared disciples, completely powerless and uncertain of the future. Then we'll see the book of Acts close with the church advancing throughout the world, proclaiming the unstoppable gospel and turning the world upside down.

No matter how fierce the opposition, no matter how bloody the persecution, every obstacle and every martyr only serves to spread the unstoppable gospel even further. There's something about its power and persistence that defies human logic. There's something about the Good News of Jesus Christ that appeals to rich and poor, powerful and powerless, Jews and Gentiles.

Again and again throughout history, people and governments have tried to intimidate believers, eradicate the church, and silence the gospel. It can't be done. The gates of hell cannot stand against the relentless advance of the church.

Let's discover how and why the gospel of Jesus Christ is *unstoppable*.

1

Mission in Motion

The Gospel's Shockwaves Are Just Getting Started

Ira Yates was born to a hardscrabble life in Hopkins County, Texas, in 1859. His father was killed when Ira was six, and his mother died when he was twelve. Orphaned at an early age, Ira and his brothers had to fend for themselves, making a meager living by digging peanuts or hiring out as ranch hands.

When Ira was nineteen, he raised cattle. He saved his money and married a preacher's daughter when he was twenty-three. In the late 1800s, that meant a dowry of prayer rather than payment. Ira tried his hand at various jobs, even serving a term as the marshal of San Angelo. In 1913, he traded 216 head of cattle for a failing dry-goods store in Rankin, Texas. Business went well, but Ira didn't enjoy shopkeeping.

In 1915, a West Texas landowner offered him thousands of acres in Pecos County in exchange for the store. Ira jumped at the chance to return to ranching, but there were huge taxes to pay and a mortgage; then droughts, falling cattle prices—and soon he was on the brink of bankruptcy.

In 1926, Ira Yates learned there was oil beneath his property. He quit the ranching business and began selling mineral rights leases to drillers from his front porch. In one day alone, he made $180,000. His in-laws' prayers were answered in bubbling black crude.

Ira Yates became an instant millionaire, and the land he owned is known today as the Yates Oil Field. That field has produced more than a billion barrels of oil since 1926. Experts believe there's another billion barrels waiting to be extracted.

For years, Ira Yates lived on the ragged edge of poverty on that land. All the while, there was unimaginable wealth right beneath his feet.[1]

The message of Acts is that we are a lot like Ira Yates. We struggle. We're never far from spiritual bankruptcy when all the resources we need are close at hand, ready to be tapped. The resources of the Holy Spirit are infinitely greater than a billion barrels of oil.

The church in the book of Acts tapped into the vast wealth and resources of the Holy Spirit—and turned the world upside down. That same power is available to us today.

The Book of Action

The book of Acts is also called The Acts of the Apostles. Perhaps a better name is The Acts of the Holy Spirit, because He is featured on every page, moving the first-century church to new miracles.

With this in mind I taught this biblical account for two years at Houston's First Baptist Church. It revolutionized our lives.

Week by week God chipped away at our hearts so that our people increasingly began to more resemble first-century Christians. We may wear Nikes instead of sandals, but we've been transformed by our encounter with people who lived twenty centuries ago.

Acts covers the period from AD 33 (when Jesus died, rose again, and ascended) to about AD 63 (when Luke wrote this book). So we are dealing with the first thirty years of church history. Charles Ryrie said that the book of Acts is "doctrine in practice. Thus the book shows us what men can do in the power of the risen Savior."[2] Acts is the sourcebook for the church in any city or century.

Though Acts contains a large cast of characters, two men dominate this book. In chapters 1 through 12, Peter is at the center. But the rest of the way—from chapter 13 onward—Paul steps into the spotlight.

The story of Acts is an account of a spiritual earthquake. Chapter by chapter, it rolls out like shockwaves from the epicenter in Jerusalem to remote geographic regions and remote people groups.

Geographic regions

- Acts 1–7: The city of Jerusalem
- Acts 8–11: Judea and Samaria
- Acts 12–28: To the ends of the earth

People groups

- Acts 2: The Jews
- Acts 8: Samaritans, who were part Jewish, part Gentile
- Acts 10: First Gentile Christian (Cornelius, the Roman centurion)

- Acts 13–28: Paul's missionary journeys take the gospel to the world

Those first-century Christians could hardly imagine how far those shockwaves would reach. To them, "the ends of the earth" meant Spain or the British Isles to the west, or the Parthian Empire or India to the east. They had no idea that the gospel would eventually be preached in the then unknown lands of China, Japan, Australia, and the undiscovered continents of North and South America.

The shockwaves of the gospel still reverberate. The story of the Acts of the Apostles is still being written. You and I are on our own missionary journeys in the twenty-first century, and we are carrying the Good News of Jesus and His resurrection into our workplaces, onto our campuses, and wherever we go.

Luke, the author of Acts, was a Greek physician and the only non-Jewish author in the entire Bible.[3] He shows us the growth and transformation of the church in its first years. At the beginning, the church appears to be a kind of para-Jewish movement, consisting entirely of Jewish people, many of whom meet for worship in the temple courts or in synagogues.

By the end of the book, the church had taken on the distinctly Christian form it has today, with such features as deacons and elders, missionary work and church planting, and meeting on Sunday instead of on the Jewish Sabbath.

We can also fully see, for the first time in the Scriptures, the triune nature of God. The Old Testament focuses on the work of God the Father. The four Gospels are about the work of Jesus the Son. And here in Acts, the Holy Spirit takes the lead.

The foundations of the early church suggest what the church today can become again. God's church has been misunderstood—including by the church itself—so this is our chance to get back to basics. Nowhere in the book of Acts do you see the word *church* used to describe a building where people gather on Sunday mornings. In Acts, the church is the people of God in love with God doing the will of God.

Throughout Acts, we see the church unstoppable as it's on the move, constantly advancing, relentlessly taking and occupying new ground. The church faces obstacles but not setbacks. The church suffers opposition but never retreats. The church endures persecution but cannot be extinguished.

New churches are planted. New lands are claimed for Christ. The church grows. And grows. And grows.

God doesn't try. God doesn't attempt. God *acts*. And His will is always accomplished. That's why this account of the early church is called the book of Acts, not the book of Tries.

If we define the church as a building or an organization, no wonder people choose to sleep in or watch football instead of getting involved. We need to restore the original biblical vision of the church as a movement, radiating into the world with a sense of power and purpose, changing lives, impacting the culture, accomplishing a mission.

We Are Theophilus

Acts is the story of how a group of ordinary people believed in the resurrected Lord, lived beyond themselves, and turned the world upside down. The first-century church set a pattern that is still the model for producing explosive results in the twenty-first century—explosive spiritual growth, explosive numerical growth, and explosive growth of ministry to the poor, orphans, widows, and prisoners. Luke opens Acts with this profound statement: "I wrote the first narrative, Theophilus, about all that Jesus *began* to do and teach until the day He was taken up" (Acts 1:1–2, emphasis added).

Acts is a sequel to the Gospel of Luke. Notice Luke speaks of what Jesus *began* to do and teach. When Jesus was taken up into heaven, His work was not completed. It would be continued in Acts as the Holy Spirit worked through the lives of the early Christians. In fact, the work Jesus *began* to do is *still* being carried out through the church today.

Both of Luke's books, the Gospel of Luke and the book of Acts, are addressed to someone named Theophilus. Who was Theophilus? We don't know for certain. In Luke 1:3, Luke addresses him as "most honorable Theophilus." Since Luke honors him with this form of address, Theophilus may have been a Roman official who came to Christ.

The name Theophilus means "one who loves God." What are we to be? We are to be lovers of God—that is, we are to be Theophilus. Loving God is the goal of the other sixty-five books in the Bible too. In a sense, Luke addresses this book to us by name to cast a vision for our lives. Our purpose in life is to be a Theophilus, a lover of God.

You may say, "No, my purpose is to be an engineer," or, "My function is to be a teacher." Well, that's your *role*, but it's *not* the purpose of your life. Consider defining yourself *spiritually* rather than vocationally. When you define yourself spiritually, you walk vocationally with a purpose. It doesn't matter if you are a nuclear engineer, an electrical engineer, a train engineer, or a sanitation engineer—your purpose in life is to be a lover of God. To become the people God intended us to be, we must shift our thinking. The greater our love for Him, the more effective we will be in our vocations as well as our relationships.

Lovers of God do and teach the will of God. They want to obey God, serve God, and imitate God. When we truly love Him, we want to do what He says. We welcome His will for our lives.

Theophilus is your destiny, and mine. I heard a true account of two next-door neighbors who had a kind of across-the-fence friendship. They loaned each other power tools, said hello, that kind of thing. One of the men was a follower of Christ and the other wasn't. When the nonbeliever lost his wife to cancer, he was devastated. He had a funeral to prepare and burial arrangements to make, and he went through all of it as if he were in a trance.

After the service, he left the funeral home and walked all night beside the river. But he wasn't alone. His next-door neighbor, a follower of Christ, also followed his friend. He never spoke. He never even walked beside him. He just followed along and watched over his friend to make sure nothing bad happened. As the sun came up, he said, "Let's go get some breakfast."

The grieving man now attends his neighbor's church. He said, "A religion that can produce the kind of caring and love my neighbor showed me is something I want to find out more about. I want to love and be loved like that for the rest of my life."[4] You and I may stumble over his use of the word *religion*, because we tend to call it a relationship—and notice how it was the relationship, not any "religion," that drew in this man, who wanted to know what made the Theophilus next door the way he was.

When people see that you, as a lover of God, know how to be a lover of people, you'll become a magnet for souls, attracting people to Christ. They're going to want what you have. They will want to become Theophilus too.

Luke has written this book to Theophilus, a first-century lover of God, and he has written it to you and me, lovers of God in the twenty-first century.

Prove It!

Next, Luke presents to us the foundation of the Christian faith and the Christian church: "After He had suffered, He also presented Himself alive to them by *many convincing proofs*, appearing to them during 40 days and speaking about the kingdom of God" (Acts 1:3, emphasis added).

I love that Luke, at the outset of this book, talks about the evidence for the resurrection. Christianity is a reasonable faith. You don't have to check your intellect at the door. You don't have to accept it by blind faith. Christianity rests on a bedrock of convincing proofs.

For those of us who have experienced doubts or questions about the Christian faith, God has given us convincing proofs and the mental faculties to consider them. So if a skeptic approaches the Christian story with a willingness to follow the evidence wherever it leads, he will ultimately find himself at the feet of the resurrected Lord.

There are many books available that offer the following resurrection proofs as well as many more. For our purposes here, let's mention four crucial proofs.

1. **The empty tomb.** Everyone in Jerusalem could see that the huge stone had been rolled away—even with vigilant Roman guards on duty. All Rome had to do was produce the body and Christianity was over.

2. **Hundreds of fulfilled prophecies.** The Old Testament virtually sings the story of a resurrected Savior, offering details of a mode of execution—crucifixion—that didn't even exist when the Hebrew Scriptures were written. Check out Isaiah 53 and Psalm 22.

3. **Eyewitnesses.** Jesus appeared to a long list of witnesses, including five hundred people at once. Hallucinations don't happen in groups. When Paul wrote about it in 1 Corinthians 15:6, many of these people were still alive to confirm it.

4. **Changed lives.** There's no testimony like firsthand experience. For two thousand years, Jesus has continued to prove He is still alive, still changing people, and still rocking the world.

I recommend that every follower of Jesus know the evidence for His resurrection. Who wouldn't want to know the details of something so wonderful, so triumphant? We can begin by majoring in the "convincing proofs" in our own lives. What has Jesus done for you? How has He brought your hopes, your dreams, and your joy back from the dead? I love to talk about our fact-based faith, but I've long noticed that when I show people what I've experienced myself, they're most likely to respond.

Luke is beginning this book by underlining that we have a resurrection faith. When Jesus was arrested, the disciples had scattered in fear and defeat. Acts is all about those very men and women coming back to life—with resolve! Not only had the forces of evil fallen short but they were going to be pushed to the brink by the early church.

This second book by Luke is itself a series of "convincing proofs" that Jesus was not only alive but now multiplied as His power radiated through His followers—to Judea, to Samaria, to the ends of the earth. Jesus was and is unstoppable. If He could defeat death, where was the limit?

Jesus proved to His disciples, in these first verses of Acts, just how powerful He was. Then He told them something just as exciting—just as ground-shaking.

He told them this power was headed their way.

Mission 1:8

In Acts 1:4, Jesus told His followers to remain in Jerusalem and wait because they were about to receive *power*—and in verse 8, Jesus reveals the source of that power: "But you will receive power when the Holy Spirit has come on you, and you will be My witnesses in Jerusalem, in all Judea and Samaria, and to the ends of the earth."

God's people must wait on God's power. Apart from the power of the Holy Spirit, we can do nothing. But once His power comes upon us, we can do *anything*. By the power of the Holy Spirit, a tiny handful of believers transformed the world forever as the gospel earthquake rumbled from Jerusalem to the ends of the earth.

The Greek word for power in this passage is *dunamis*, from which we get our English words dynamo, dynamite, and dynamic. The Spirit fills us with God's dynamite! He empowers us, as His church, to do amazing things.

What is the Lord's plan for the limitless power He will pour into us? He is sending us out on a mission. He is commissioning us to go, to be His messengers locally, nationally, and globally. Jesus says He is empowering us and authorizing us to be "witnesses in Jerusalem, in all Judea and Samaria, and to the ends of the earth." Because Jesus sends His church out on this mission in Acts 1:8, I call God's plan for the church "Mission 1:8." That phrase has become a statement of identity and destiny for our church in Houston.

I began sensing the Lord leading me to a vision for Houston's First that would be greater than we could ever imagine. This idea of following the Acts 1:8 pattern and reaching out to our city, our nation, and our world began to take root. Our church desired to expand with multisite locations. We also partnered with our denomination to champion church planting in the

United States. We were already sending out over twenty mission teams a year to different parts of the world but we wanted to help plant churches internationally too.

How could we tie all of this together into a cohesive strategy? The vision for that came to me in what I call my San Francisco Moment.

My family and I were on sabbatical in San Francisco, staying at Golden Gate Baptist Theological Seminary. Each morning I would walk up the hill to the student center. The prayer room in the student center offers a postcard-perfect view of Sausalito, the Bay Bridge, Alcatraz, and the San Francisco skyline. On my knees in a sunlit room in California, I would spend hours in prayer, asking God to crystalize the vision for Houston's First Baptist.

One morning, the fog precluded my view and I sensed the Lord saying to me, *Gregg, your view of San Francisco is like your vision for Houston. You know the city is there, but you can't see it through the fog. I have a vision, but you just can't see it right now.*

The next day the view was a little clearer, but it was still somewhat obscured. But the third day was amazingly crisp and clear. I could see the gleaming buildings of the city across the Bay—and in that same instant, I saw my vision for Mission 1:8.

I realize that the foggy weather of the Bay Area was symbolic of my heart. My vision was cloudy, and I needed to keep going back to my knees to find clarity.

I took this vision home—and this vision began to make a difference in our city, our nation, and our world. Our heart was to plant two multisite campuses in Houston, identify three cities in the United States and three cities internationally to partner with church planters in the next twenty-four months. We would also reach out with renewed purpose to the poor, the widows, the orphans, and the prisoners. The words of Jesus in Acts 1:8 became Mission 1:8, impacting our church in a powerful way. We set a goal of raising $60 million in two years. Our existing two-year budget was $45 million, and we decided to raise $15 million more for the additional vision.[5] Many people thought we were crazy. One highly respected ministry rep said point blank, "That's impossible."

Can you imagine how our faith grew as the challenge increased? It would have to. Nothing but God's power could get this done, so if it happened, we'd know where the power had come from. Mission 1:8 and radical generosity captured our church as our journey in His power began.

It became clear to us that the words of Jesus in Acts 1:8 were not directed merely to a handful of disciples in Jerusalem in the first century AD. He is still speaking to us today through those words as we read them. He was challenging the church in the first century— and He is still challenging the twenty-first-century church today. Jesus is saying, "I'm sending you on a mission—Mission 1:8. I'm sending you with My full authorization, in the power of the Holy Spirit. You will be My witnesses, My messengers, and you'll start here in Jerusalem. Then you'll move out into Judea (the surrounding region), and into Samaria (the border region), and then you'll carry My message to the ends of the earth."

We live in amazing times. We can carry out Mission 1:8 by hopping on a jet plane and flying to the ends of the earth. We can carry out Mission 1:8 by sending the Good News out to the ends of the earth over the internet. And we can carry out Mission 1:8 right at home, because the world is literally coming to our cities. Whenever you go to work, to school, to the store, or anywhere else in your town, odds are you'll hear unfamiliar languages being spoken—Spanish, Portuguese, French, Vietnamese,

Chinese, Arabic, Farsi, and on and on. In this amazing age, and this wonderful "melting pot" called America, we can carry the Lord's message to the ends of the earth without ever leaving our hometown.

Did you know there are thirteen million people in North America who don't know a single Christian? That's one in five non-Christians. You might not think that could be possible in this country, but welcome to the modern world. And when we think of specific groups, the numbers are even more staggering. Among Buddhists, 65 percent don't know a Christ-follower. Among Hindus, it's 78 percent, and among Muslims, 43 percent have no acquaintances who can tell them about Jesus. A new study tells us these things, and Todd Johnson, who helped with the research, suggests this: invite a family to share dinner with you. Bring them into your home for Thanksgiving. Small gestures can be the biggest, because that's when people can see Theophilus in us.[6]

The first-century church didn't receive anything that you and I don't already have. We received the same power they had on the day we became Christians. We received the dynamite of God so that we can carry out Mission 1:8. Now our work extends from our doorstep to the ends of the earth.

Many of us have been living like poor Ira Yates before he knew there was oil under his feet. Many of us live as if we are spiritually bankrupt. But in Acts 1:8, Jesus tells us that all the resources we could ever want or need are within easy reach. The wait is over. The Holy Spirit has come. If you have trusted Jesus Christ as your Savior, then *you have received power.*

You and I have the power to do whatever it is that God wants us to do. And we already know the first thing He wants us to do: tell the world about Him.

A little boy once heard that if he asked Jesus to be his Savior, God would come live inside his heart. So he asked his parents, "How can God live inside my heart? He's so big! He made the whole world! If he lived inside my heart, he'd stick out!"

That little boy was right. If God truly lives in our hearts, he's going to stick out. His power will stick out. His love will stick out. His forgiveness will stick out. If God truly lives in our hearts, He will stick out locally, He will stick out nationally, and He will stick out globally.

The power of the Holy Spirit is dynamite. You just can't contain the explosion, and you can't keep it quiet. Jesus is calling you and me to make that explosion—the most joyful one in history—as big as this world.

Theodore Williams, missionary to India, once said, "We face a humanity that is too precious to neglect. We know a remedy for the ills of the world too wonderful to withhold. We have a Christ too glorious to hide. We have an adventure that is too thrilling to miss."[7] And the great Scottish evangelist and Bible teacher Oswald Chambers said, "The thing that makes a missionary is the sight of what Jesus did on the cross and to have heard Him say, 'Go.'"[8]

Mission 1:8 is an adventure too thrilling to miss. Our Lord has said Go. He has commissioned us to be His witnesses at home, across our land, and to the ends of the earth. We are the church. We have received power. We are His mission in motion.

2

The Power Line

The Force That Moves God's Hand

May I bare my soul for a moment?

As Mission 1:8 took off in our church, I felt the Lord urging me to ramp up prayer in my life through fasting. I began to fast at least a meal a week, and it's become a lifestyle.

Occasionally, I miss a week, but my goal still is to fast at least one meal per week, usually breakfast, sometimes breakfast and lunch. I devote the extra time to prayer. This initiative has developed greater spiritual discipline in my life.

Fasting is not just a matter of going without food. It's a matter of going after God. It's not just an attempt to "will" my way through physical hunger but a statement: "Lord, I'm taking this physical need, and I'm making it symbolic of my spiritual need for You. Lord, I am fasting for You. I'm fasting for the church. I'm fasting for my family."

I came to the further conclusion that God wanted me to do what's called a "Daniel Fast." This comes from Daniel 1:8–16. Daniel resolved that he would not defile himself with the food and wine provided by the king of Babylon. Instead, for ten days Daniel ate only vegetables and drank only water.

So, when observing my Daniel Fast, I ate only that which came out of the ground—fruits and vegetables, baked potatoes, whole grains—and drank only pure water. No meat, no dairy products, no sweeteners, no butter or sour cream on the potatoes, and only a little oil and vinegar on the vegetables. I felt the Lord was calling me to observe a Daniel Fast for ten days, and my wife, Kelly, joined me in this. Symbolically, I fasted to celebrate what God had done in our lives and in the church during the first ten years of my pastorate. I also wanted to pray for the next ten years of what God was going to do. I prayed for my wife, my children, my church, and myself.

It was hard. It was especially hard during the first few days. But Kelly and I kept to our commitment. And I will tell you, when you're fasting, and you are praying for the future of your children, it impacts the way you pray. And when you're fasting, and you're praying for your church, it impacts the way you pray. It takes you to a new place in prayer. It takes you to a new depth of commitment to God, a new depth of relationship with God.

Please understand, as God has searched my heart, I am not telling you this in order to brag or impress anyone. I am not willing to lose any eternal reward just to impress people. But I felt God calling me to let you into this part of my relationship with Him, in the hope that it would inspire and challenge you to go deeper with God.

So I ask you: If it takes eating a plain baked potato and a plain salad night after night for more than a week to see God work in your own heart, in your family, and in your church, isn't that worth it? Isn't that more valuable than a sandwich and chips and a glass of iced tea? What are you willing to forgo in order to see God at work? What would you be willing to do, what would you be willing to endure, what would you be willing to give up in order to experience greater depth in your prayer life?

Prayer is power. God can change hearts and circumstances through the power of prayer alone. We need to continually go deeper with God in prayer—and we need to teach our children, by word and example, what it means to daily seek the Lord in prayer.

In Luke 11, the disciples said to Jesus, "Lord, teach us to pray." Not teach us to preach or plan or lead. "Teach us to pray." Why did they say that? They wanted Jesus to teach them to pray because He had shown them through His example that prayer was the beginning of all things good. They had seen Jesus pray many times—sometimes when He was among them, sometimes when He withdrew from them and prayed alone. They knew that He went out late at night and spent hours in prayer with the Father.

So, after walking with Jesus and observing His example, they said, "Lord, teach us to pray."

We tend to think of prayer as a passive activity. It seems like we aren't *doing* anything. We're just talking to God. But authentic prayer is anything but passive. Prayer is action. Prayer is work, and it demands our time and sacrifice. Prayer is not for the slacker—it's for the achiever. And prayer results in action that pleases and honors God. It connects us to the Power that created the universe.

In the book of Acts, we see that whenever the first-century church prayed, God moved. Prayer unleashes the limitless power of God.

Ten Days That Shook the World

As Acts begins, Jesus has returned from the dead but has yet to ascend. He spends time with His disciples, teaching them to wait in Jerusalem for the coming of the Holy Spirit. He also gives the marching orders to take the gospel near and far— what we've referred to as Mission 1:8. Then they watch Him disappear into the heavens, with that mandate fixed in their minds.

Luke calls these remaining eleven disciples *apostles*, meaning "people sent out on a mission." Now they know what the mission is. They must have thought deeply about it as they returned to Jerusalem, as Luke describes. He tells us they adjourned to an upstairs room where they were staying together—the eleven, now that Judas Iscariot was no longer with them: Peter, John, James, Andrew, Philip, Thomas, Bartholomew, Matthew, James the son of Alphaeus, Simon the Zealot, and Judas the son of James.

Here's what we know about how they spent their time: "*All these were continually united in prayer*, along with the women, including Mary the mother of Jesus, and His brothers" (Acts 1:14, emphasis added).

We don't read about them planning a service, doing some preaching, or assigning casseroles for a potluck supper. Instead they closed the doors and began to pray—and not just for an hour or two. No, they "were *continually* united in prayer." When you read through Acts, you realize that Luke, as a physician, writes with prescription and precision. If he says they were "continually in prayer," he means *constantly*.

Soon, very soon, the church is going to launch out on an epic expedition to new worlds. But before they take a single step, the first official act of the early church is prayer.

Let that sink in. No song or sermon, no offering of donations or establishing denominations, no focus on man but on God. Their top priority was prayer. The early Christians connected to heaven before getting started on earth.

Pentecost was ten days away. That's when the promised gift of the Holy Spirit would finally arrive. From the ascension of Christ until the day of Pentecost, we find a ten-day waiting period in which the apostles and the other disciples do one thing and one thing only: they pray.

Ten days of prayer, I can testify, is harder than it sounds. Our ten-day Daniel Fast was a greater challenge than I anticipated. My body became weak even as my heart was full. Through the fast, I lost ten pounds—not that weight loss was my goal. I'm a lean, small-framed man, and I didn't have ten pounds to lose.

Here's an entry from my journal on day eight at 9:50 p.m.:

> The fast has moved from inconvenient to hard. . . . All day I have been sniffling and sneezing. Eating this healthy is making me sick. Ha! I trust this is all for the great and eternal good. Please Lord, hear our prayers and shower down your blessing, will, favor, and truth.

There were sniffles, stomach pangs, and weakness. But those things were momentary, while the lessons I learned will be with me everywhere I go for the rest of my life.

Start with Prayer

There are a number of principles we can learn from the disciples' ten-day prayer meeting.

1. Prayer is primary.

Prayer was the first thing the disciples did once Jesus left. For many of us in the church today, prayer is not primary—and often not even secondary. Prayer is often a last resort: "When all else fails, pray." When we have exhausted all other options, we fall to our knees in desperation, calling out, "Dear Lord, help us! Rescue us! Pull us out of this pit we have dug through our prayerlessness!"

But prayer was not the last resort of the early church. It was not even the first item to open the agenda. Prayer *was* the agenda. The apostles came back from the Mount of Olives, went straight upstairs, shut the door, and prayed.

2. Prayer is a matter of forethought, not an afterthought.

Prayer needs to be consciously, deliberately prioritized and scheduled into our day. It's a very short distance between an afterthought and no thought. I suggest you schedule your days according to this pattern: *pray, plan,* and *proceed.* Does that sound a little obsessive-compulsive, a little Type A? That just may be so; I only know that it works for me.

Start your day with prayer, asking God to reveal His plan, His agenda for your day. Ask Him to make you sensitive to the "ministry of interruptions," the things that suddenly break into your schedule. If you didn't plan them, there's a good chance God did, and these are ministry opportunities.

Then, after praying and listening for the voice of God's Spirit, plan your day. Make it a flexible plan, so you can respond to unplanned events. Grant yourself some margin instead of packing the day from start to finish. Then, once you have prayed and planned—proceed. Live out your day based on the foundation you have laid.

I confess that I don't always operate by the pray, plan, and proceed method. But I can honestly testify that my most rewarding, effective, satisfying days always begin by that principle.

Most of us operate by the opposite principle: proceed, plan, pray. Our schedules are running us, rather than the other way around, so we don't even try to get on top of things. And prayer? Maybe once things calm down. So we proceed, jumping right into the workday without talking to God, thinking, or planning. We check our email and Facebook before we ever think to bend our knees to God. Then we wonder why the day wasn't satisfying, why we never seemed ready for anything, and why God seemed so quiet.

Once we get into a mess, then we try a plan—then, as an afterthought, a prayer: "Lord, please bless this plan. I know I haven't consulted with you all day, but I'm asking you to just make it all work somehow."

It's difficult to stumble around blindfolded all day then expect to step right onto the path of God's will. Better to look for it first thing in the morning, then draw the map, then set out. Again—I just know it works best for me when prayer is forethought and not afterthought.

3. Fear can be a great motivator.

Why did the early church begin with prayer? Why did the apostles and other believers join together in constant prayer? Was it because the early believers were such spiritual giants? No! They joined together in continuous prayer because they were shaking in their boots.

The Romans had crucified their Lord—and maybe they were next. Prayer is life when you're scared to death. Nobody likes fear, much less admitting to feeling it. But when we go to our knees in fear, we rise up in faith.

We may not fear for our physical safety, as the disciples did, but we make up for it in emotional and social anxiety. I know what it means to fear failure. Even writing this book, I wonder whether it will change lives—or end up in next weekend's garage sale. And that drives me to prayer, for this writing, or for whatever my heart may fear.

What are you afraid of? The prospect of divorce, something concerning the kids, a report from the doctor, the loss of a job—all of these are things God wants to take up with you. Fear breaks down the pride that keeps us from running to Him, and for that reason, I appreciate it.

Let God know exactly how you feel. Don't dress it up or pretend—what's the point? God knows your heart, and He wants you to give it to Him as it really is so that He can strengthen it.

Fear and faith are like the opposite ends of a child's seesaw. When fear rises, faith falls. When faith rises, fear falls—and prayer is the fulcrum on which all of it balances. Shift your balance to the faith side.

4. Prayer unites us.

Do you notice that verb, *unites*? Acts 1:14 says the disciples "were continually united in prayer." The original Greek text tells us that the apostles and other believers were not merely gathered together—they were *unified*. In other words, the early believers were single-minded. They were completely on the same page. Why? Because prayer unites us. As a group, we bring all our separate thoughts, emotions, and agendas, and God gives all of us His to share. It's an amazing feeling to have that strong of a connection to other people.

It only happens, however, when we commit to God's path rather than ask Him to sign off on the ones we've devised. We have to remember who is serving whom. *What can we do for you, Lord?* Once we ask a unified question, we become a unified people. Then amazing things begin to happen.

The reason for so much disunity and disharmony in the church is that so many Christians contend for their own agendas, not God's agenda. When we pray together and seek God's will together, He will unify us and keep us focused on our common center, which is Jesus the Lord.

When the early church adjourned to that upper room, there weren't Peter prayers and Matthew prayers and John prayers. There were *God* prayers, revolving around Him and His purposes. These were the same disciples who had, in the presence of Jesus, argued about who would have the highest placement in the kingdom of God. The Holy Spirit changed all that. He had them praying about the highest service to the kingdom of God.

We do a whole lot of praying at our church. On a normal Sunday, we have twenty or more people walking the rows in prayer forty-five minutes before the first service starts, interceding for those who will soon be worshiping there.[1] During the service the prayer rails at the front are open, and every six weeks we have prayer partners standing in front of each section of seats to pray with people as we worship through song—we make it a point to remember we're not merely singing; we are worshiping through song and prayer.

The house of prayer should drip soaking wet with prayer! Often I'll pray on my knees during the service. Sometimes people remark to me, "I've never seen a pastor get on his knees to pray during a service." Personally, I think it's strange that this is something new to them. Prayer in worship, for worship, should be the norm. Maybe I'm just more fearful than other pastors, but I'm afraid of leading a service in which we give less than our best to the Master.

A church based in prayer is also a place where people feel connected to each other. It is so encouraging to connect in prayer and to know in tough times that someone is going to spiritually "have my back." A church that continually connects with God will be interconnected and unified as well.

One Among Many

Acts 1:15 tells us that, in those days when the early church was joined together constantly in prayer, the entire Christian church consisted of about 120 people. At our church in Houston, we have Life Bible Study classes bigger than that. Yet that tiny assemblage of people would soon turn the entire world upside-down.

Those 120 believers were quite a diverse group. From the biographies we know, we can point to a tax collector (Matthew), a political radical (Simon the Zealot), a few blue-collar fishermen, a Greek (Philip), and a pessimist (Thomas). Simon of Cyrene, from North Africa, was probably there, and it's reasonable to think a Pharisee such as Nicodemus was among them. There were also women, an inclusion that was unusual in that era. And there were the friends and family of Jesus Himself. The poor and the wealthy, Jews and Greeks, men and women, the unquestioning and the skeptical, brothers, sisters, and mothers—only one possible thing could have brought such a group together, in that century or any other. The love of Jesus was that thing.

This is the genius and beauty of the Christian church. *All* are invited. All agendas are checked at the door other than what we share in Christ.

Sometimes people ask, "Why do you go to church with people who are so different from you?" We reply that in Christ, we are utterly compatible brothers and sisters. The distinctions melt away because we are centered in Him. We all agree that we want to "minimize me and maximize Thee" (see John 3:30).

At an Urbana missions conference, which is held for college students every third year, something amazing happened not too long ago. Thousands of students come to Urbana from all over the world, and this particular year they were studying John's Gospel and the theme, "God with us." After the main sessions they'd move to small prayer groups. There was a group of Chinese students in one area, and also groups of students from Taiwan and Hong Kong. Dividers were placed to separate the groups—a visual reminder of the tremendous conflict among those nations. But one evening the members of the Chinese group had a request for their leader—they wanted to invite the other groups to pray and worship with them.

At first only the Taiwanese accepted the invitation. The wall was removed, and the groups began to sing hymns and pray together. After a while, the Hong Kong students felt their reservations melt away; they came in too. "We're living out what we learned this week," said one Chinese girl. "This kind of thing could not happen in any other situation."[2]

It happens virtually nowhere else—but it's the beauty of the church praying. There are no walls to separate people. There are no ceilings to shut off heaven. There is only a strong foundation in the Word of God.

We stress this idea in our congregation. There's not a black church and a white church. There's not a church for people in suits and a church for people in jeans. There's not a church for the young and a church for the old. There is one unified church. When we bring our beautiful diversity together around the dynamic center of Jesus Himself, the church becomes an unstoppable freight train of Good News, proclaiming the gospel of Christ.

If you haven't felt the unity of shared praying, you can't imagine what you've missed. How do you get started? I suggest you begin praying with your spouse and your kids—not just for them, but with them, holding hands with them, putting your arm around them, and joining with them in prayer. What a great way to build family unity! Think about what might happen to those little family tensions and conflicts if you began to do this every day.

Are you a husband? Trust me—your wife will love it when you pray with her. It may be a little uncomfortable for some men at first, but they quickly become comfortable with seeing the delight in their wife's face.

Teenagers need to hear their parents call out their names to heaven. Why is it that we would willingly die for them yet we seldom pray with them? We crave true unity and togetherness yet it doesn't occur to us that coming before God is the best way to achieve that.

You may be single, or you may be someone who wants to expand your prayer adventure. Find a prayer partner in your church, workplace, or neighborhood to meet with weekly, or to pray with over the phone (or even via text or email—God honors any approach). Here's a challenge: find someone who is totally different from you in political views or economic status or profession, and pray together for unity, saying, "Lord, please minimize me and maximize Thee." Then watch the unity begin to bind you together.

And why is it we don't think to be creative and comprehensive with something as crucial as prayer? For instance, our ministerial staff members and their spouses have church members acting as prayer warriors assigned to pray for them. They meet at least once a month to exchange prayer requests. And I've had the same prayer partner for more than ten years—a lawyer more than a decade and a half older (and a foot taller) than me. He has prayed for me *every day* for more than a decade. We are different people, bound in prayer. I can't begin to express how grateful I am for his prayers, and the church's prayers, for Team Matte.

Life most often unravels because of some kind of dissension, disharmony, or disunity—in families, in churches, or in friendships. In every single case, prayer is the solution because it is the supreme bonding agent. It dissolves friction, builds love, and glorifies God. And in this global village that increasingly throws different kinds of people together, we need prayer more than ever. We need to know how to love, how to serve, and how to build God's kingdom through these new relationships coming our way.

What decision or dilemma are you facing? My advice is to start praying, listening for the still, small voice of the Holy Spirit within you. Prayer is your connection to the power of God, so pray *big* prayers. Don't stop at asking Him to solve a problem—call on Him to accomplish *mighty* things through you, through your family, through your church. It's been said that we cannot pray a prayer so big that God will not wish we had prayed for something even bigger.

Phillips Brooks, the Episcopal clergyman who penned the Christmas carol "O Little Town of Bethlehem," once wrote,

O, do not pray for easy lives. Pray to be stronger men! Do not pray for tasks equal to your powers. Pray for powers equal to your tasks! Then the doing of your work shall be no miracle. But you shall be a miracle. Every day you shall wonder at yourself, at the richness of life which has come to you by the grace of God.[3]

I felt something like that on day ten of my Daniel Fast. Like a runner at the end of his biggest race, I was tired, weak—and jubilant. In my journal, I wrote these words:

We made it! Thank you, Lord! It was tough, inconvenient, and a builder of discipline. . . . I'm trusting that the Lord will answer our prayers. I didn't have big "warm fuzzy" times with Him. It was a spiritual discipline, but I trust it was more than physical. I desired, and still do desire, the eternal more than the tasty. Yes, Lord, to the next ten years!

3

Going Global

God's Power Unleashed through the Church

Neither the birth of a child nor the birth of a vision is easy, but both are enjoyable—once they're over!

A central part of our Mission 1:8 was birthing multisite locations in our city of Houston. Our primary site is the Loop campus, located in the southwest corner of the interchange between I–10 and the West Loop (I–610 West).

We'd originally been a downtown church before moving to the Loop in the 1970s. Now we were back. A few years ago, we'd started a second campus in the bottom floor of the office building that had been built on our former site. Like a heart beating in the chest of our city, our downtown site pumped the lifeblood of the gospel to people we could never have reached before. I loved the way our past and future were intertwined in creative mission.

That was only the beginning. Now we were planning to birth *two* new campuses on one day—Easter. Our new Sienna

Campus to the south involved adopting a struggling church in a retail center. And our new Cypress Campus to the north involved hauling chairs, audio-visual equipment, and other gear in a fleet of trailers into a middle school cafeteria. Those two campuses of our church—one adopted and one born—joined our family fifty miles apart on the same Sunday.

On that Easter, our church proclaimed the empty tomb from four campuses instead of two. Five Sunday services became nine. We knew there was no turning back; this was an unstoppable initiative. Yes, the problems of administering a large multisite church are very complex. But in a congregation of faith and vision, those are the problems you *want* to have. And I have enjoyed every—well, *almost* every minute of it!

The act of birthing a church is beautiful, exciting, and painful all at the same time. This is true whether the church being birthed is a new campus in twenty-first-century Houston, Texas, or the original church in first-century Jerusalem. Acts 2 shows us the ultimate maternity ward for churches. Everything we do now started then and there.

Jesus had tried to prepare His followers for what lay ahead, but they had slept through some of the Master Teacher's lessons and argued through others. He'd told them the Holy Spirit was coming. He'd told them something incredible was afoot—that they would take His message to the ends of the earth (Acts 1:8). Even the prophecies of the Old Testament had been telling them these things. God loving the world, God sending a Savior, that Savior blessing the entire earth—all of it was spelled out, down to the last nail on the cross, if they were paying attention.

But they weren't. What the people of that time wanted was a military uprising. They wanted a political empire with a messiah on the throne. God's people had very clear-cut ideas about how

God should go about His work. They simply didn't think big enough, wonderful enough, or loving enough. They couldn't have foreseen the awesomeness of God's grace until it fell on their heads like a combination of a hurricane and a wildfire—one the size of eternity.

Birth, Wind, and Fire

Jesus had left His disciples with a promise: they were to wait in Jerusalem, and they'd receive power from the Holy Spirit—power to take the gospel throughout the world. For the next ten days, they prayed, and God prepared them for the explosion. They were a handful of Jesus followers, about 120 in number, but not yet the church. Something else had to happen before they could lay claim to that status. By divine appointment, it would happen on the day of Pentecost.

> When the day of Pentecost had arrived, they were all together in one place. Suddenly a sound like that of a violent rushing wind came from heaven, and it filled the whole house where they were staying. And tongues, like flames of fire that were divided, appeared to them and rested on each one of them. Then they were all filled with the Holy Spirit and began to speak in different languages, as the Spirit gave them ability for speech. (Acts 2:1–4)

Let's notice three things that happened on this historic day.

1. God's timing.

Jesus was slain on Passover, not by coincidence but by way of highlighting the fact that Jesus is our Passover Lamb. Before the exodus from Egypt, the blood of the Passover lamb was splashed on the doorposts of Jewish homes so that the angel of death would "pass over" those homes and leave everyone inside unharmed. The blood of Jesus, our Passover Lamb, was shed on the cross and is sprinkled on the doorposts of our hearts so that the wrath of God may pass over us.

Fifty days after the Passover we arrive at Pentecost, the Feast of Weeks, commemorating the giving of the Law on Sinai—still celebrated in Judaism as Shavuot. Amazing. The church was born in the power of New Testament grace during a celebration of Old Testament law. I thought about that as we started our new downtown church on our old site. God loves tying the past and the future together in a message of His grace. And He loves punctuating His message with wonderful timing.

We become impatient too often, thinking that God is "taking His time" getting to what we want. We should be grateful that it's *His* time, because it comes with His love and wisdom. He knows exactly what we need, when and how we need it. Day forty-seven might suit our schedules, but God knows it must be day fifty. Wisdom comes in learning to wait on God, to trust in His timing.

Pentecost was no arbitrary choice for what God had in mind.

It was a feast day, fifty days after Passover. It also served as a harvest festival. What God had planned was a harvest of souls from the nations. Jerusalem was at peak capacity at the moment when the Good News of Jesus Christ would be launched as a worldwide movement, in every language and for every people group.

2. God's power.

Acts tells us, "Suddenly a sound like that of a violent rushing wind came from heaven, and it filled the whole house where they were staying" (v. 2). Here in the Gulf States—not only in

Texas but in Louisiana, Mississippi, Alabama, and Florida—we understand the concept of "violent wind." This is hurricane country, and every few years we receive a powerful reminder. A hurricane knocks down anything that tries to stand against it.

No hurricane filled the house at Pentecost—just the sound of one, according to the text. God wasn't demonstrating destructive power but *creative* power—the same creative force we see in Genesis 2:7, where we read about the creation of humanity from dust.

The Spirit of God came with the sound of a violent wind but with the creative power of God's breath of life. The breath of God—the Spirit of God—breathed spiritual life into them, and the church was born.

God is giving us a picture of the conversion experience. You don't ease into Christianity by gradual stages—you are completely born again. It's a radical transformation, a function of God's power.

In John 3, Jesus explained this idea to Nicodemus, the curious Pharisee, and pay attention to how He describes being born again: "*The wind blows* where it pleases, and you hear its sound, but you don't know where it comes from or where it is going. So it is with everyone born of the Spirit" (John 3:8, emphasis added). The Spirit is compared, once again, to a creative wind—the breath of life—yet it is as powerful as a hurricane. He breathes life into a dead church.

Paul writes to Corinth describing the deadly gales of God's power that uproot idols and strongholds, "blowing" them away. He says our weapons are "powerful through God for the demolition of strongholds. We demolish arguments and every high-minded thing that is raised up against the knowledge of God, taking every thought captive to obey Christ" (2 Cor. 10:4–5).

Over time lies and false teaching spring up like weeds, but they're no match for God's power.

We'll see this time and again in Acts: the power of God toppling idols. In those days, these were generally statues and shrines. Our idols today may be less obvious but they're just as false and deadly: idols of fame, wealth, success, sex, and pleasure. God's rushing wind, blowing through your life and mine, knocks down the idols in our lives.

3. God's presence.

Acts tells us, "And tongues, like flames of fire that were divided, appeared to them and rested on each one of them" (Acts 2:3). If wind is a biblical image for the power of God, fire often symbolizes His presence. We see the same principle in the Old Testament. God spoke to Moses from a burning bush, and God led the people of Israel by a pillar of fire by night. Fire purifies, so it also gives us the idea of God's purity. His presence burns away the impurities in our lives, leaving the powerful steel of Christlike character.

But not often enough. Not in every church. Not in every life. All too often, God's timing, power, and presence are nowhere to be found among us. We are impatient with God's timing and intoxicated with our own self-important schemes and schedules. We figure we have the power to get things done, just based on our skill and talents. We'd rather do it our way than wait for His. But God is teaching us that His timing precedes His power.

In Acts 2, the Holy Spirit arrives in God's timing, God's power, and God's presence. And a firestorm is released upon the world.

Those who study natural phenomena tell us about one of the most terrifying spectacles of nature: the firestorm. When a flame burns with enough intensity, it creates its own wind system. In other words, it is a conflagration with storm force. Fire plus wind is a deadly combination, with the power and fury of fire riding on the wings of a heavy wind. If the right elements come together at the right time, a firestorm will rage. It can destroy vast forests and entire cities.

We see this mighty force in Acts, but in the hands of a wonderful God. The fire of His presence is combined with the wind of His Spirit, on the divine schedule, and the resulting flame leaps into the world. Twenty centuries later, the burning continues.

This insignificant little band of Jesus followers, at this moment in history, became the church. And we still are. Today, in the twenty-first century, the power and presence and timing of God are spreading like wildfire through those of us who are fully committed to Him.

The age of Mission 1:8 continues. We are witnesses for this moment, locally, nationally, and globally. God is still on the move.

Validation—Not Communication

The incredible show wasn't over yet. Acts 2 tells us that those present were filled with the Holy Spirit and began to speak in different languages. A curious crowd of observant Jewish pilgrims from many nations quickly formed, and they began to pick out their own native languages in the commotion. Luke gives us a list of the nations and languages that people were hearing.

The bewildered spectators said, "We hear them speaking the magnificent acts of God in our own languages" (Acts 2:11).

Luke goes on to tell us that everyone was astounded and yet, as we would expect, there were cynics and skeptics who suggested they'd come upon a drunken party (see v. 13).

Imagine all those human languages discoursing on the same subject: "the magnificent acts of God." Diversity of tongue, unity of theme.

Over the years, "speaking in tongues" has been debated in various quarters of the church. Here is what we know about the languages the disciples spoke on the day of Pentecost. These believers were not just uttering sounds they could not understand. They were declaring the wonders of God (possibly Old Testament miracles) in the known and listed languages of various peoples of the earth.

When the disciples spoke in other languages, God was sending a message: the whole gospel for the whole world.

Genesis 11 holds a key to understanding this narrative. It's the story of the Tower of Babel. The people had come together, all speaking one language, with the intention of building a tower that would reach to heaven. The people wanted to make a name for themselves. But God thwarted their arrogant intention by causing their unified language to be turned into many languages, so that the people could no longer communicate and cooperate together. Because of this, the people were scattered and their tower was left unfinished.

Now, on the day of Pentecost, the Holy Spirit of God has come among the disciples in Jerusalem, and He has reversed what took place at Babel. He has shown that the gospel of Jesus Christ will be a worldwide gospel, a gospel of all peoples, a gospel that knows no boundaries. Languages had been a wall between people: Jesus was and is an unstoppable force to knock down walls.

A Global God, a Global Message

These events we see in Acts 2—the sound of a rushing wind, the tongues of fire, the profusion of languages—are nothing less than miracles. The Scriptures call these phenomena "signs and wonders." Signs and wonders are not given to us as mere special effects to sensationalize God's work. Signs and wonders in the Scriptures serve a specific purpose: *they validate the works of God.*

The various languages spoken on the day of Pentecost were not given to enable people to communicate with each other. They were given to validate the work God was doing that day in breathing life into the newborn church. The religious pilgrims in Jerusalem had come from the four corners of the known world to celebrate the feast of Pentecost, but few of them had a language problem. The Jews who lived among other cultures were, for the most part, bilingual—they spoke both Aramaic (the common language of first-century Hebrew culture) and the language of the country they lived in.

Later, we will see the apostle Peter speak to all of the people in Aramaic. Everyone will understand him because he speaks the common language. Though the Jewish people were scattered across the known world, they were unified by culture and language.

Up to this point, God's program in history has been focused on the Hebrew people. Here in Acts 2, God demonstrates that He is doing something bigger than even the nation of Israel can contain. The Good News of Jesus Christ is for all nations.

What does this event say to us in the church in the twenty-first century? It tells us that we can't let language be a barrier. There are roughly 6,500 languages in the world today. It's true that a third of them are spoken by groups of less than one thousand,[1] but it's also true that God wants the Gospel preached to *everyone*, in *every* language. What if people from around the world could come into our churches, access an earpiece, and hear the Good News in Spanish or Vietnamese or any of the other languages spoken in our communities? What if they could come into the youth program or singles ministry and hear the gospel in their own cultural vernacular?

In Acts 2, God is saying to us, "I am going to great lengths to show you that I am a global God with a global message." The message of Jesus Christ is for all people. We have an incredible opportunity to go to anyone from anywhere and say, "This is for *you*. God did this for *you!*" We need to span the languages.

But we also need to span other divisions. The gospel is for everyone in every situation. It's for alcoholics and addicts who seek deliverance, adulterers who seek to repent, divorced people who seek acceptance, financially broken people who seek a second chance, widows and widowers who seek consolation, guilty offenders who seek forgiveness, teenagers in search of their true identity, and the physically and mentally ill who seek healing in their lives.

For all these people we have Good News. For all those who are old but also those who are young; for all those who are poor but also those who are rich; for men and women, for married and single, for every color and variety and personality, there is the best possible news, and the church brings that message on the fire and the wind.

A few years ago I urged everyone in our church to go on a mission trip. I was thinking internationally, of course, but across the street would also have worked. What I was really after was seeing people cross boundaries and leave their normal context.

Because once we do that, things begin to happen. We realize we are missionaries, whether we like it or not, and all those little rules and roles that keep us from sharing our faith at work fall by the wayside.

I always benefit from stepping outside my safe little bubble of everyday existence. I encounter people who are vastly different from me yet strangely the same. I may not understand their language, but I totally understand their love for their kids. The commonality of the human soul transcends all the variances and cultural distinctions that would keep us from understanding one another and loving one another.

God gives each individual Christian and each church a distinctive vision to fulfill. Houston's First Baptist Church is now made up of four campuses, each one unique—yet we are all Houston's First Baptist Church, through and through. All four campuses were born in different ways, all four reach different communities, and all four serve the same Lord and proclaim the same unstoppable gospel. We all shout a loud "Yeah!" to the creative varieties of God, and a loud "No!" to the cookie-cutter sameness of man.

These things are exciting to me, and our new vision is thrilling. But as one of our staff members has said, "Where there is vision, there is work." And I can't help but notice that the more the vision grows, the more the work expands with it. The church, by my reckoning, is entering a new era of creativity and willingness to break down barriers. What we're doing at Houston's First is also occurring in other cities and other nations. We may have a pleasing brand name for it—Mission 1:8—but it's a very old product. God actually branded it before time even began to tick away. It was only a matter of His timing, His presence, and His power to come together.

We didn't start the fire. God did, and Acts 2 tells us all about it. What counts now is fanning those flames so that they spread in every direction. And maybe a few of us need to set ourselves on holy fire, because, as someone once said, when we set ourselves aflame the whole world will come to watch us burn.

4

All Roads to the Cross

Why Jesus Is the Answer to Every Question

Here's what I notice about people who get things done: they tend to use to-do lists. They prioritize a guide for the day, then follow it and stay on task.

I also notice how to-do lists express the personalities of those who use them. Creative personalities decorate with doodles. Pragmatic types make lists that are plain, functional, and simple. Young hipsters keep lists on their phones. And hectic, messy folks use what I call the "to-do tattoo"—illegible notes scrawled on wrists or hands with a ballpoint pen.

Personally, I'm just a straight-up post-it note/mobile phone guy. Sometimes I enjoy my list so much I'll write a task down I've already completed, just for the satisfaction of checking the box! I know it's crazy, but if you're type A, you understand.

But here's the best of all. My favorite to-do list is one kept by an intensely focused personality. This list that has *one* action item on it: "Today I will: _____." End of list.

You and I, we crowd our lists. We accomplish a lot of peripheral tasks and check them off, yet we neglect our highest priority. The cure for a lack of focus is to put only one item on the list, and focus on nothing else until that one is 100 percent done.

Peter is a one-item guy in Acts 2. He's going to bring the first sermon ever delivered in the Christian church. He has one point: "Preach Jesus." No "thanks for having me," no jokes or poems or family stories—just Jesus.

The sermon will end with a to-do list that is just as focused, but now it's the audience's turn. They're going to leave with one action item. Not a bad communication strategy. Let's see how it works.

Why the First Shall Last

The Holy Spirit has launched His great work on earth with a show of power—the sound of a mighty wind, tongues of fire, and the miraculous ability of the believers to speak in languages from around the world. Naturally there were some who scoffed—the disciples had been drinking, they said.

Now, I don't know about you, but I have never heard a drunkard begin telling the wonders of God in Cantonese or French. Drunken, slurred English does not make someone bilingual.

The enemies of the gospel still look for rationalizations when the truth is staring them in the face. They'll propose any crazy theory rather than confront the truth that Jesus is on the move.

Peter sees the smirking, and he steps forward to speak—in Aramaic, the language of the Jews who are the skeptics at the moment. But he speaks to us in many languages. If you've been raised Catholic, you know he is considered the first pope—so listen. If you grew up in Judaism, you hear how he quotes the sacred Hebrew law—and he'll open your eyes to its meaning. If you've been raised in no tradition at all, Peter is here to teach you about the roots and reason of the Christian church. In other words, whoever you are, the first Christian sermon is of first importance.

What Binds the Book

Luke, in Acts 2:14–36, gives us the text of Peter's sermon on Pentecost. I won't quote Peter's entire message here. Instead, I can sum up his message this way: everything that has just taken place—from the tongues of fire to the disciples speaking in many languages—serves to fulfill the Old Testament prophecy of Joel. In fact, all of the Old Testament prophecies point to Jesus as the long-awaited Messiah.

After Peter has finished building an irrefutable case for Jesus the Messiah from the prophecies of Joel, he aims for the heart of the crowd. Peter has one action item on his to-do list, so listen closely as he checks that box and delivers a "come to Jesus" invitation with deadly power:

> Men of Israel, listen to these words: This Jesus the Nazarene was a man pointed out to you by God with miracles, wonders, and signs that God did among you through Him, just as you yourselves know. Though He was delivered up according to God's determined plan and foreknowledge, you used lawless people to nail Him to a cross and kill Him. God raised Him

up, ending the pains of death, because it was not possible for Him to be held by it. (Acts 2:22–24)

Peter is saying this: Has Jesus been crucified? Absolutely, but only by the deliberate plan of God. This was no setback for Him—the cross and empty tomb can be found in the ancient Scriptures every Jew knows. A band of thugs may have done the dirty work—and they would pay for it—but they had no idea they were serving the cause of heaven.

I'm fascinated by this passage because it holds two theological views people tend to set against each other: the sovereignty of God and the responsibility of man. The cross was "God's determined plan," yet lawless people killed Him. In other words, God is in control, but the men involved are held responsible. That question of seemingly contradictory thoughts has been debated for centuries, but Peter puts those two factors side by side on the table.

He also quotes King David from Psalm 16:10: "For You will not abandon me to Sheol; You will not allow Your Faithful One to see decay." We know King David wrote those words, then died and, yes, decayed. So these words must have been pointing to someone else: Jesus Christ.

The first Christian sermon about Jesus is filled with Old Testament references. Why? Because the Old Testament is filled with Jesus references. The entire Bible is about Jesus. The Old Testament is filled with prophecies, *Christophanies* (appearances of Christ), and symbols of Jesus to come. The New Testament reveals the fulfillment of all of those Old Testament prophecies and the life of Jesus, who came and is returning again.

From Genesis to Revelation, it's all about Jesus. He is the beginning, middle, and end. He is the one who binds our Bibles together.

Call and Response

I have no idea whether Peter's sermon preparation was anything like mine. Since he stepped forward to preach spontaneously, and since the Holy Spirit had only just arrived—probably not.

As for me, it's three to four hours a day, three to four days each week. I spend that time reading, researching, praying, and listening for a heavenly whisper.

On some days, it seems like sermon preparation is all I get accomplished—while other times it seems like Sundays are only three or four days apart instead of seven. Yet I really love the challenge of taking a passage of Scripture to its depths, and finding a way to apply it to our daily lives. I often tend to pack too much information into the sermon out of fear of coming up short.

But I've learned that, whatever the subject or text or occasion, all roads should lead to the cross and the empty tomb. It's the great subject of all preaching, and Peter already understands this. He begins in Joel and the psalms and he ends up at the cross and the empty tomb. You can start nearly anywhere, but there's only one destination.

In structuring his sermon, Peter has followed a simple to-do list with only one action item: get to the cross and the empty tomb. There has been one theme with one character: Jesus.

Is that true in today's church? In many quarters of the church, it seems we hear a lot about how to be fulfilled, how to overcome anxiety, how to fix our marriages, how to raise our kids, how to get out of debt—and yes, the name of Jesus is often appended to that message somewhere. But the message is not really *about Jesus*. It's not about who He is, what He did, why He suffered, or what it means that He rose again. Jesus has become just the vehicle leading us to some personal goal that may be a fine goal, but secondary to the main event.

I understand the heart behind not coming on too strong. But with the problems in today's world, we desperately need eternity's Answer. Seeking to effectively fulfill the Great Commission, the vision of our church is to be a "Relevant Biblical Community."

Relevant reaches out to culture, *biblical* impacts souls, and *community* connects our people. The church needs all three, but we seem to be drifting to building relevant communities short on biblical truth.

That's a club, not a church. Especially not the church Peter is starting. Jesus must be the center of our message and ministry.

One of the nicest—and saddest—compliments I receive is, "Thank you for teaching the Bible and talking about Jesus. So few churches do that anymore."

I'm glad to hear that the message has been helpful. But . . . thanking a preacher for talking about Jesus? That's like thanking a baseball pitcher for throwing a strike. Isn't that what we're supposed to do? Jesus is the message. He isn't the backdrop. He is the Way, the Truth, and the Life.

Peter will end his sermon with an assignment—a one-item to-do list. He calls for a personal, logical, and heartfelt response to what he has just shared:

> When they heard this, they came under deep conviction and said to Peter and the rest of the apostles: "Brothers, *what must we do?*"
>
> "Repent," Peter said to them, "and be baptized, each of you, in the name of Jesus Christ for the forgiveness of your sins, and you will receive the gift of the Holy Spirit. For the promise is for you and for your children, and for all who are far off, as many as the Lord our God will call." (Acts 2:37–39, emphasis added)

The conviction of sin demands a response. When you know you have sinned, when you know you are under judgment, you realize your need of a Savior. That's the realization Peter's message has stirred in these people. So they want to know: What should we do in response?

A great sermon isn't a collection of information; it's a *call to action*. When people have heard a preacher deliver a great sermon, they will not say, "That was nice," and go home with their minds on something else. They'll have to *act* on what they have heard. They'll need to jump up, run out, and leap into the fray. True preaching convicts, motivates, energizes, and moves its hearers to *action*.

In his book *Everyone Communicates, Few Connect*, leadership expert and former pastor John Maxwell tells a story about Abraham Lincoln. The president attended a church close to the White House every Wednesday night. The pastor, Dr. Gurley, allowed him to sit in a special study with the door open, where he could hear the sermon without causing too much fuss.

One night, Lincoln was walking back to the White House after Wednesday preaching. A friend asked him what he thought about the sermon, and Lincoln said, "Well, it was brilliantly conceived, biblical, relevant, and well presented."

"So, it was a great sermon?" asked the friend.

"No," Lincoln replied. "It failed. It failed because Dr. Gurley did not ask us to do something great." He of all people knew that the purpose of communication is to inspire action.[1]

Cut to the Heart

No one left Peter's sermon nodding, smiling, and picking up where they left off an hour earlier. The original language for "deep conviction" here tells us these people were "cut to the heart." That's the target of our ministry. The heart is where our treasure is, where our control panel lies.

Peter's hearers didn't merely feel bad, or ashamed, or chagrined. They were in deep pain. They realized for the first time what it meant to have rejected and crucified the Messiah, and they were suffering in that knowledge. They had to do something.

The Greek poet Homer uses this same word to describe horses stomping and pounding their hooves. To be "cut to the heart" is to feel as if a horse has trampled you and burrowed its hoof into the flesh of your heart. As Christians, we can't be afraid to cut people to the heart with the truth of God's Word. If I need heart surgery, I don't want my surgeon to be afraid to cut close to my heart. I want him to use his scalpel fearlessly and save my life.

The word *conviction* makes us a little uncomfortable in church today. Encouragement? Application? Oh yes, we're eager to deal in those things. But conviction? We don't want to scare anyone away. Our numbers might take a hit. The collection plate may come back lighter. So we find ourselves telling people what they want to hear rather than what they need to hear.

We can't abandon our calling, which is to give people the gospel. And the gospel is surgical. It cuts to the heart, and we should be hearing people say, "Brothers, what must we do?"

A recent guest at our church sent me an email, telling me how, one month earlier, he had decided to walk away from church, from religiosity, from God Himself. He was uncomfortable because he was feeling under conviction. He simply couldn't handle the weight of it, so he tried to step back into the life he'd once had, before Christ—the friends, the places, the habits. But it wasn't the same. He couldn't go back "home" again, because he saw through the whole masquerade. The Holy Spirit wasn't going to let go of him, and though the truth hurt, it was still truth. So he came back to God and dealt with the conviction. "What God provides is real," he wrote. "What the world provides is an imitation."

Conviction moves us to run to God. Peter's preaching caused those skeptics to plead for guidance: "Brothers, what must we do?" They were ready to receive Peter's one-item list, and he gave it to them: "Repent and be baptized."

But wait—isn't that *two* items? (1) Repent. (2) Be baptized.

And another question: Peter seems to call for baptism as a way to be saved—or does he?

We shouldn't read too much into his comments here. Baptism doesn't save us; it's an *outward symbol* of the salvation we have already received by grace through simple faith. When Peter says, "Repent and be baptized . . . for the forgiveness of your sins," the original Greek word translated "for" is *eis*, which can *better* be translated "because of" or "on account of." Peter is actually saying (and this would be more clear in the original Greek), "Be baptized *because* your sins have been forgiven." Peter is calling for baptism *on account of* the salvation his listeners will receive by faith, upon repentance and the acceptance of Christ.

The one item on Peter's list, then, is *repent*. The people are already halfway to repentance, because repentance begins with conviction. Peter's sermon has made that happen. The sword of the Spirit cuts to the heart. The goal of biblical preaching is not to make people feel guilty or condemned but to open their hearts to *the conviction of the Holy Spirit.*

What's the difference between condemnation and authentic conviction? Condemnation makes you feel worthless and it paralyzes you. When you feel condemned and riddled with guilt, you say to yourself, *I'm no good. I always mess up. I can never measure up as a Christian.*

But conviction is specific and focused. Conviction makes you aware of specific sins, attitudes, and habits in your life that need to be changed. Though the conviction of sin is painful for a growing believer, our souls desire the conviction of sin because our Christian growth and life depend on it. Condemnation immobilizes; conviction motivates. Condemnation leaves you hopeless; conviction gives you hope in Christ. Condemnation makes you want to hide from God; conviction prompts you to run to Him.

Condemnation is a thing of the past for Christians. "Therefore, no condemnation now exists for those in Christ Jesus" (Rom. 8:1).

Some from Peter's audience had been in the crowd that shouted to Pontius Pilate, "Give us Barabbas!" and "Crucify Him!" After word had spread of the Lord's resurrection, some had probably walked out the city gates and visited the garden tomb—the tomb where the body of Jesus had been sealed by Roman guards, the tomb that now stood open and empty. What were their thoughts?

Every Sunday I talk to people who sense the Holy Spirit's conviction. After they repent—utter relief! Secrets and sins make you sick. But forgiveness brings freedom; repentance brings relief. Bringing our secrets into the light and offering them to God is liberating. It adds years to your life—not to mention eternity.

A Change of Mind

The final words of Peter's sermon are not only convicting but devastating: "God has made this Jesus, *whom you crucified,* both Lord and Messiah!" (Acts 2:36, emphasis added). Imagine how those in the audience must have felt—those who had the blood of God's Son on their hands. No wonder they were so urgent in asking what to do—how to deal with their guilt, how to rinse away that blood.

Peter replied, "Repent . . . and be baptized, each of you, in the name of Jesus Christ for the forgiveness of your sins, and you will receive the gift of the Holy Spirit" (v. 38).

The Greek word translated "repentance" is *metanoia*, which literally means "after-mind" or "changed mind." To repent is to change the way you think about your life and your behavior. It means to change your thinking, change your heart, and change the direction of your life. It is agreeing that God is right and we were wrong. So Peter tells his listeners to repent and reverse the course of their lives.

Natural regret isn't the same as the repentance God makes possible. As human beings we can feel natural shame and be disgusted with ourselves. But left to our own devices, we get over it and return, sooner or later, to our old vices. The Bible offers quite a collection of guilty individuals, but only five of the ten who confess, "I have sinned," move forward to repentance.

- King David: 2 Samuel 12:13
- Nehemiah: Nehemiah 1:6
- Job: Job 42:5–6
- Micah: Micah 7:9
- The prodigal son: Luke 15:18

Others acknowledged their sin but refused to leave it at God's feet. What about you? Confession is only the first step. True repentance is humility before God, resulting in a change of our thinking that transforms the core of our living. Repentance means an about-face in the way we've been living. We'll struggle. We'll be tempted. But we're moving in the opposite direction.

Those who repented after hearing Peter preach made a complete break with their old way of life and adopted a *new* way of life. Their hearts cried out to God in repentance.

To repent does not mean that you will become morally perfect and sinless ever after. But we can go to God and say, "I want to turn my life around and walk away. Save me and live Your life through me."

Some people imagine a balance scale in heaven, with good deeds on one side and bad on the other. If we can just tip the scale with 51 percent good stuff, we've got it made. The problem is that God doesn't look for 51 percent. He wants 100 percent purity. This is why only Jesus, who lived a flawless life, can save us. Try as we might, we can't save ourselves. We can't attain perfection—not even for one day.

Jesus exchanged His purity and perfection for our sin and stain. He died on the cross to make that exchange, then rose again as the pioneer of a new resurrection life. We confess our sins, repent of them, and accept the gift that God offers us through His Son. This is why Peter offers a sermon with one call to action: *repent* in order to accept Christ and be saved.

I once heard about a man who felt deeply convicted of sin. He came forward at the end of a Sunday morning worship service to offer a prayer of repentance. He went to his knees, and his pastor knelt beside him. "Lord," the man prayed, "remove the cobwebs of sin from my life."

His pastor put his arm around the man and added, "And kill the spider, Lord."

When we pray and repent of our sin, let's be sure that we not only ask God to remove the cobwebs of sin but also ask God to kill the spider as well—to remove the sin itself, not just the guilt from it.

Many Questions, One Answer

If Peter has one directive, to repent, he really has one subject, one reason—Jesus. He is really the answer to all the big questions. Questions about salvation? Jesus is the answer. Questions about Christian living? Jesus covers them. Questions about death? About everyday problems? About marriage that endures? Jesus.

And what about the church?

People try to make the church be about many things: a political movement, social justice, personal success and motivation, country-club life. But the answer is none of the above. The church is all about Jesus. Anything else is not the church. And that should alarm us because we see so many churches today that are about everything *but* Jesus. The very reason for their existence has slipped away. Notice Peter's progression: first Jesus is clearly declared, then he calls for conviction, repentance, and life change. Maybe the lack of life change in our churches needs to be traced back to the lack of Jesus being central.

How do you find a new church? Do you evaluate its programs? How entertaining the preacher is? The band or choir? My suggestion is this: attend a few services or check them out on the internet, and listen to see if this church is talking about Jesus. If not, the location doesn't matter. The programs don't matter. The friendliness and music don't matter. You have one item on your list, and that item is Jesus—if you're looking for the authentic church.

Imagine a steakhouse with a wonderful facility, comfortable seating, great service, beautiful menus, a pleasing ambience, and parsley on the plate—everything but steak. In the church, Jesus is the steak. He's the main course and the only course. If he's not on the menu, you're going to be hungry when you leave.

Don't think I'm negating or diminishing ministry. We lift Christ high in order to meet the true needs of the soul. But the goal of church is not to make earth a nicer waiting room at the door to hell. The church exists to reroute us to heaven by way of Jesus. We become focused on meeting particular needs, but if we don't do that through the power and blood of Jesus, we're simply passing the time, putting on a nice show. We are here to show the hope of Christ as a relevant biblical community.

We all have our issues, but whatever they are, Jesus is the answer. The closer we come to Him, the better we know Him, the more we allow Him to guide our lives through the power of the Holy Spirit, the more these issues seem to fade away.

A few years ago there was a Vietnam veterans' parade in Chicago. The old soldiers carried a tremendous banner that, like the memorial in the nation's capital, bore the names of all the soldiers who had died in that war. A news team was on the scene, and the reporter approached one of the soldiers and asked him why he had traveled so many miles to be a part of this parade.

The soldier was in tears and could hardly talk, but he pointed to a name on the banner and said, "Because of this man right here. He gave his life for me. He gave his life for *me*." And as he spoke, he wasn't looking at the reporter but at the name, which he kept tracing over and over with his finger. The camera zoomed in on that and faded to the image of the soldier weeping and running his finger over the letters of a name—the

name of a man who had died for him. He couldn't get over the
fact that he was alive and at home because of what someone
else had done for him—and all he could do was continue to
trace that name.[2]

That's what we do in the church. At our best, we realize
what Jesus has done for us, and we can't quite wrap our minds
or emotions around it. The whole thing is just too powerful,
too wonderful, and church is the place where we come to trace
that name with our lives, our minds, and our work. We may go
down this road and that one, but they all lead back to the cross.

You'll always find us tracing His name, tracing His hand,
then following where He wants us to go. But when we find that
we're caught up in disputes, when we find that we've lost our
power or our focus, I would suggest to you that the problem is
not marketing nor advertising nor location. The problem is that
there's not enough Jesus. The problem is that the parade is still
marching but we've forgotten what's on our banner.

Whether you're a member or a leader or just someone not
too sure about this whole church deal, I would suggest you
check the Jesus quotient. Is your church all about Him? And if
not, start asking how that can be changed. Make sure He's the
center and focus of your church and your life.

One Sunday after church, I was relaxing with my cute-as-a-
button elementary school–age daughter. As little children often
do, she said something to me that was amazingly wise: "Daddy,
you don't know everything about Jesus." (It also sounded a little
smart-alecky, to tell you the truth.)

"You're right, Valerie, I don't," I replied, wondering where
this was going.

"You know some things about Jesus, but not everything."

"Yes, I know some things, but not everything."

Finally, the moment of sweet childlike wisdom: "But Daddy, Jesus knows *everything* about you."

Awww. "Yes, Valerie, He does."

I don't know everything about Jesus, but He knows me and He loves me anyway. And because He loves me, I love Him. And because He loves the church, and gave Himself for it, I love the church. The church—if it is truly and authentically and biblically the church—is all about Jesus.

That is what the first pope preached, if you are Catholic. That is what a Jewish fisherman proclaimed, if you are of Hebrew descent. And that is what a follower of Jesus, an eyewitness to the cross, and the first preacher on Pentecost taught us: first, middle, last, and always, our message is Jesus.

To-do: "Today I will live—*for Jesus.*"

5

Love in Three Words

Why the Church Exploded

As I prayed, I wondered: *Would God say yes? How could He say no? What do I even want? What are Kelly's thoughts as a mom?*

We prayed with open hands and open hearts. We asked God if he wanted us to adopt a child. We had the money, the heart, and the connections. We knew that, as the church, we're called to care for orphans; the question was *how*.

If we were going to adopt, it had to be the Lord's will, not just an emotional whim after watching a video on adoption. Taking a child into our home would not be a small matter. Not only would this decision irreversibly impact the life of a child but it would have a permanent impact on our family and my ministry.

You might be surprised—I know I was!—that the Lord's answer to our prayer was *no*, but I distinctly heard God place a comma after the word *no* when He answered our prayer. What did that comma mean?

God was *not* simply telling us, *No. Don't adopt.* He was saying to us, *No, I want you to use your position to send thousands in your place*, though I was not caught up in numbers. What was important was the idea God was planting within me.

If Kelly and I had adopted a child, I would've found myself focused intensely on that child and our birth children, Greyson and Valerie. And as a parent of an *adopted* child, that *should* be my focus.

But my role as pastor enabled me to focus on mobilizing, equipping, helping, and welcoming countless families. I saw a vision of our church as a beacon for orphans, as well as a strong support and foundation for adopting families. I knew what God was calling me to do.

Houston's First has a long tradition of taking up a benevolence offering on days when we serve the Lord's Supper. So the next time we served communion, I shared my vision with the congregation. A number of families in our church with adopted children stood behind me as I spoke. I felt the wonderful weight of standing for the orphans as I talked about this need—and I felt the tears coming as I tried to talk about it.

Somehow, I managed to tell the congregation that our goal was to raise $100,000 that day—yes, you read that number right—to provide adoption aid grants to families to help them shoulder the heavy financial burden of adoption.

By day's end we had received a total of $87,000, an amazing sum only $13,000 short of our goal. The next Sunday I shared the total and said, "I think the $13,000 is here. How many of you knew the Lord was speaking on Sunday but forgot to act on it by Monday? Let's do it."

By the following Sunday we had received more than $180,000 for our adoption fund. I was shocked by the landslide of generosity—yet I was not surprised that we had more than met our goal. I knew God was leading us in this direction, and where God leads, He also provides.

Jesus has commissioned us to share His Good News locally, nationally, and globally. And one of the ways we can share the gospel and share His love is by adopting children into our families. He has sent us on a mission. Our life's purpose through His church is to bring more people into the family of faith. It's a mission of prayer, a mission to care, and a mission to share.

All In

The early church had a problem. The crowds saw that resurrection power was at work, something even more incredible than what they'd seen Jesus do in the flesh. And they wanted in. The leaders had to be very practical in caring for the great influx of new believers, spiritually and physically.

The close of Acts 2 is one of the most triumphant passages in all of Scripture:

> And they devoted themselves to the apostles' teaching, to the fellowship, to the breaking of bread, and to the prayers.
>
> Then fear came over everyone, and many wonders and signs were being performed through the apostles. Now all the believers were together and held all things in common. They sold their possessions and property and distributed the proceeds to all, as anyone had a need. Every day they devoted themselves to meeting together in the temple complex, and broke bread from house to house. They ate their food with a joyful and humble attitude, praising God and having favor with all the people.

And every day the Lord added to them those who were being saved. (Acts 2:42–47)

It's clear that many of the people who came into the church had physical and financial needs. So those with extra shared with those who lacked. Out of their common love for the Lord Jesus, they came together and shared meals, praising God together and enjoying each other's company.

And everyone who came into the church adopted the mission that Jesus had given His followers on the Mount of Olives—Mission 1:8. They shared the Good News of Jesus Christ with their unsaved friends and neighbors. As a result of their vibrant witness for Christ, "every day the Lord added to them those who were being saved" (v. 47). They were spiritually adopted into the Father's house.

So the church was truly unstoppable—though you'd better believe some were trying to stop it. The people were serving Christ, and when that happens, the world shakes.

Three Steps toward Heaven

In this brief description of the early days of the first-century church, we see a powerful threefold process for growing the church, whether in the first century or the twenty-first century. Those three steps are prayer, care, and share.

1. Prayer.

Luke tells us that the early Christians "devoted themselves to the apostles' teaching, to the fellowship, to the breaking of bread, and to the prayers" (v. 42). Every great vision from God starts with prayer and is confirmed by prayer. At the World

Missionary Conference in Edinburgh, 1910, Dr. George Robson said, "We shall need three times more men, four times more money, and seven times more prayer" to evangelize the world.[1] It's clear where he placed his priorities.

Prayer is the key to effective evangelism. Before you stop and have a conversation about Christ with your neighbor, your co-worker, or a fellow student—pause for prayer. It doesn't need to be long and involved. It's enough to say, *Lord, let me speak your words.*

Instead of merely taking an exercise walk through your neighborhood, take a prayer walk. Pray for the people who live in the houses in your neighborhood. Pray for their spiritual, emotional, and financial needs—and pray especially for their salvation. Ask God to do His work in their lives, and ask Him to use you as His chosen instrument in your neighborhood. My wife and I have seen a couple of our neighbors come to Christ as a result of our prayer walks, and we continue to pray for others in our neighborhood. See yourself as the pastor of your block. God put you there deliberately. Pick out three or four houses around you to pray for and get ready for open doors of ministry.

Also pray for your church. God has strategically placed that body of believers in that location to have an impact on your community. Pray your church will shine like a beacon in the night to people who need Christ. Pray for the leaders of your church, that they would maintain their humility, purity, boldness, courage, and commitment to the Mission 1:8 ministry of the church.

Every pastor is in deep need of prayer. Far from being spiritual superheroes, we are human beings dealing with the best and worst events in people's lives, and our job is never done. Pray for us to have soft hearts, wise heads, and thick skins.

Ask God to show you where He can use you in your church as a witness for Him. Encourage the leaders.

A friend of mine says, "The reason we don't pray is not because we're too busy but because we're too confident." Let's be on our knees in humility, knowing we need Him every hour.

2. Care.

Luke shows how the believers cared for the needs of one another. It's an incredibly moving picture of the church living out its divine identity. Caring for people is the best possible way to open a conversation about Jesus Christ. It has been said that people don't care how much you know until they know how much you care. When people see your sincerity, they trust you and listen to you.

I'm not suggesting you should use "caring" as a tool of manipulation. Caring is not just an evangelistic technique. We care because it is right, because God cares. And even if and when people reject the gospel, we continue to care just as He does.

Can you imagine the infinite choices for being creative in caring? Because it's what God wants us to do, He makes sure we're at our best when we look for ways to care. Wherever you are, you're probably surrounded by people. Revive the lost art of caring. Do something completely unexpected to serve the needs of someone else.

The early church embraced the ministry of caring—and they embraced one another. They were engaged and involved in each other's lives, and when someone had a need, a brother or sister in Christ was there to meet it. The twenty-first-century church needs to recapture the caring spirit of the first-century church. That means we need to stop staring at our smartphones and start noticing the people around us—especially when they have needs.

3. Share.

The cycle is complete: we pray, and we're led to care. We care, and we're led to talk about Jesus. "Let me tell you why I can love at all," we say. "It's because Jesus first loved me." And then we can talk about the many wonderful attributes of our Savior; how He is the Way, the Truth, and the Life; and how no one comes to the Father but through Him.

It may not always happen in this precise, 1-2-3 order. But this is a pretty good template. Prayer opens the door to eternal life for others. We talk to God, we love others, and we connect them to God—a beautiful circle of God redeeming humanity. And the best part is, it can become an incredible, dynamic lifestyle.

In most cases, sharing Christ will be built on the foundation of a friendship. When you follow this three-step process, you'll find that every interaction sends you through the process again—prayer, care, share. You'll pray for someone and find some way of demonstrating your authentic caring—even if it's just to say, "I've been praying for you about that problem you shared with me; how is that going?" The Lord will give you some opportunity, some opening to share with that person how Jesus is the answer to whatever he or she is going through.

The next time you see that person, you begin again with prayer, then find how you can care, then as the door opens you'll be able to share. Repeat and repeat again.

Your cycle may last weeks, months, even a decade or two. Maybe you'll see the seeds sprout, and maybe not. But you'll know you're an obedient servant and that God is blessing your efforts. Maybe someone else will finally lead your friend to Christ. The results and the glory belong to God, but the joy of praying, caring, and sharing is all ours.

Strengths and Weaknesses

Prayer, care, and share: Which is your favorite? Which is the hardest? You'll find that all of us have our specialties. Based on our spiritual gifts, we'll differ in where we excel and where we're more likely to struggle.

I tend to love the third step. I simply love talking about Jesus, so just hand me the microphone, point me to a platform, and turn me loose. Invite me on a mission trip, and show me the people. I'm highly verbal and evangelistically driven—that's my comfort zone. Others love to closet themselves and pray for hours, and they do it like warriors. And I know people who have the gifts of hospitality and caring, and they're incredible at helping others.

While our strengths differ, we all need to own the process. That is, the evangelism part may seem scary to you, but you don't want to miss that joy. The truth is, I might be too comfortable in that role, and therefore depend less on God. Your humility about sharing, on the other hand, would lead you into a great victory because you would pray hard and depend completely on Him for your words and your strength. For that very reason, we need to be sure we get outside our comfort zones and do those things that *aren't* part of our gift set.

My second-favorite step is prayer. I love talking to the Lord and waiting to see how He'll respond in opening a door for me to share Christ. But I have to confess that caring, the next step, is the toughest one for me. I can and will do it, but I have to *remind* myself to do it.

Gifted leaders aren't always gifted caregivers. They may even struggle with compassion. Does that mean they should just steer clear of compassion? Of course not! *All* these traits are for *all* of us. We just need to give more effort in certain directions. Leaders like me want to look down the road and focus on goals, but God's process of molding us into the image of Christ will involve chipping away at that until we become more conscious of the needs in our circles. Someone once told me that megachurch pastors often love "the machine," but they don't love the people who live inside it. That statement took root in my soul, and I've asked God not to let our church become so much cold machinery. We're called to become a force of love and caring in our urban community, and that's where we've set our vision.

God has also helped me grow personally in the area of caring. I work at it. I ask God each day to make me more sensitive to opportunities to show the compassion and love of Christ. As many times as possible in the course of a day, I say, "What can I do to help?"

So it can be done. You can be good at the thing you're not good at! Our goal is always Christ, who was a perfect 10.0 in all three categories. You can do studies in praying, caring, and sharing as recorded in the Gospels, and you'll see how He exercised each to perfection. We won't reach His levels, but we can aim at them.

So don't say, "That's not my thing." Ask God to make you an even more versatile servant of His kingdom. Dare yourself to go about your life this very week and focus on your point of challenge.

And remember: once you're cycling toward sharing Christ, know that this is the last thing Satan wants to happen. Also remember: this is the *unstoppable* gospel—so he is doomed to fail. But he'll take his shot. He'll tell you the time is wrong, you're not ready, the other person is going to be offended, or you'll be tongue-tied.

When that frequency starts coming in, change the station. The Holy Spirit is always broadcasting, and you simply need to be tuned in to His message. He's going to encourage you. He'll tell you it's always the right time to serve Christ, and you're as ready as you'll ever be because His power and presence go with you. He'll say, *Just let me do the talking, and you show the love.*

Expect Satan to major on the parts you don't like. If you'd love to stay in care mode all the time but are afraid to take that final step and speak the name of Christ, he'll tell you something like this: *If you really care, you won't take the risk of offending.* There's a phrase often attributed to St. Francis of Assisi: "Preach the gospel. Use words when necessary." Caregivers love that one, because it seems to imply they can go on forever "preaching" without actually saying anything. The problem is that people need to know the reason we care. They need to know the name of Jesus, and they need to know how to be saved. Ed Stetzer puts it this way: "Preach the gospel and since it's necessary, use words."[2] I think it's wonderful that some have the compassion for marathon caring (care-athon?), but I want to urge those people to "pop the question" at some point. Close the deal. Let them know the reason for your caring and ask for a response.

For the prayer warriors—we couldn't make it without you. Thank you for your persistence on your knees. But we also need you out here on the front lines occasionally. Caring and sharing with those for whom you pray will help you pray more intelligently and passionately. As the prophet Isaiah said, "How beautiful on the mountains are the feet of the herald, who proclaims peace, who brings news of good things, who proclaims salvation" (Isa. 52:7).

If you are a follower of Christ, He has called you to a lifestyle of prayer, care, and share. Just as surely as the risen Lord Jesus commissioned Peter and the other apostles on the Mount of Olives, He has commissioned you. He has given you a gift for true excellence, but He also wants you to have the adventure of rounding out your talents.

An Unstoppable Hug

We cycled through at Houston's First, and here's what happened.

We prayed about orphans, and our caring deepened until we had to do something. That caused us to share—to proclaim—the Christian duty of caring for orphans. Today, many Christian parents are fulfilling that vision, caring and sharing their homes with children who had none. As I write these words, our people have given more than $700,000 toward adoption aid grants to help make adoption possible for Christian families. Our church has assisted in the adoption of more than one hundred children.

These kids are both foreign and domestic adoptions. More than 30 percent have special needs, and some are adopted by missionaries around the world; all these children are precious in God's sight. Let me tell you about just one of the families God has blessed through our church.

Wes Mathew is a self-employed businessman whose family originally came from India. Kasey, his wife, is a pastor's daughter and former schoolteacher. They're part of our congregation. In June 2009, Wes and Kasey went on a short-term mission trip to the tiny Baltic nation of Latvia, where they worked at a summer camp for orphaned children.

The Mathews had been talking about adoption for some time. Their plan was to wait until after they had biological children. But their hearts changed after they'd spent time with those love-starved Latvian orphans. On the trip home, Kasey said, "I don't think we should wait to adopt."

Wes said, "That's exactly what I've been thinking."

They began the application process for adopting as soon as they got home. The social worker for their case suggested they apply to India. In 2010, Wes and Kasey touched down in India to meet and bring home their three-year-old daughter, Priya Grace.

Though all children want a loving home, it's not easy for a child to give her trust to two strangers who say, "We're your mommy and daddy." When Wes and Kasey took Priya out of the orphanage, she screamed and struggled as if she were being kidnapped. That night in the hotel, Wes and Kasey wanted to hug their new daughter, play with her, and bond with her—but Priya would only sit sullenly on the bed, staring at them.

By the next morning, however, she began to open up and play with Kasey. Soon they brought Priya home. It wasn't long at all before they were making plans to adopt a second child from India.

It's an expensive process to adopt a child, so Wes and Kasey stockpiled money in their adoption fund. But this time it was harder. Many discouraging months passed and no referral came. Paperwork had to be renewed and the costs soared, even though there was no guarantee that they would receive a referral.

In January 2013, Wes developed a mysterious illness that doctors couldn't diagnose. He lost forty pounds in a month. As Wes's medical bills mounted, they had to draw from their adoption fund. A referral to a child could come at any moment, but if their funds were depleted they'd have to turn the child down.

The doctors never figured out what was ailing Wes. But by February, he was beginning to feel better and he was out of the hospital—but the family adoption fund was now almost nonexistent. That month they attended church and something amazing happened. During the service they found out the congregation was going to gift them with an adoption grant. The Mathews and two other families were surprise recipients at our service. There were tears and laughter at church that day.

The amount of the grant was $15,000. What neither I nor anyone else at the church knew was that this was *precisely the amount that Wes's medical emergency had drained from their adoption fund*. God had their backs all along. He was glorified through the way He met their needs, when they had no power to meet them on their own.

Less than two weeks after our church gave the adoption aid grant to Wes and Kasey, they received a referral from an orphanage in Delhi. Their second daughter was a shy five-year-old girl who had been abandoned in a market; they named her Hope. On March 27, 2014, she became part of the family, and Priya gave her new sister a stuffed bunny and a hug that just wouldn't stop.

Before and after: Hope in India (L); Hope with her family: Wes, Kasey, and Priya Mathew

Prayer. Care. Share. Three little words, and they even rhyme. You could say this is God's music for the soundtrack of our lives together—the beautiful melody of people being loved into the kingdom of God. The model was set two thousand years ago, recorded in the book of Acts, and plays out every day as Jesus continues to do miracles throughout the world through His body, the church. Next verse, same as the first.

Let your church become a symphony of praise.

6

For Us, Not from Us

Secrets of the Generous Heart

Let me tell you about another family in our church.

A mom, a dad, and their little boy were sitting at the dining room table. The boy piped up, "Are we going on a mission trip to Cambodia anytime soon?"

Both the mom and the dad nearly choked. "Cambodia?" the mom said. "Why did you ask about Cambodia?"

"I don't know," the boy replied. "Just wondering."

"Well," the mother said, "we're not planning a mission trip, but it's funny you should mention it. I've actually been praying for Cambodia this week."

The father said, "And it happens that I was just talking to somebody at church who's going to Cambodia on a mission trip. He told me they have an opportunity to take food into

Cambodia to feed the poor. For about twenty dollars, you can buy enough rice to feed a Cambodian family for a month."

The boy thought it over for a moment, then said, "I think God wants me to raise money to buy food for people in Cambodia."

"That's great!" the father said. "Why don't you go and pray about it? Ask God to place a number on your heart. Then, when you know how much money God wants you to raise for Cambodia, come and tell us."

The boy went to his room and prayed for a while. Then he came back and said, "God wants me to give fifty dollars. And I'm kind of mad about it."

"Well," the father said, "that's usually how it works. You ask God for a number, and He gives you a number that's more than you think you can handle. That's called *faith*. I'll tell you what, son—whatever you raise, I'll match. If you raise fifty dollars, I'll put in another fifty dollars. That way, every dollar you raise will buy two dollars' worth of food."

The boy was motivated by that idea. He set up a lemonade stand and raised about thirty dollars selling lemonade, then he washed cars and raised another twenty dollars. He produced the fifty dollars, his father matched it, and they sent a total of one hundred dollars with the mission team from our church. That donation fed five Cambodian families for a month.

How do I know this story so well? Simple. The dad in the story is me. The mom is Kelly. The boy in the story is our son, Greyson.

But my favorite part of the story hasn't even come yet. There's more.

Some time later, the Cambodian families sent thank-you notes and photos to Greyson. He treasured those mementos, and Kelly decided to have them framed for Greyson's wall as a reminder of the importance of generosity.

When Kelly took the mementos to the framing shop, the man at the counter said, "I have a boy your age. You must be very proud of your son for wanting to help other people. I wonder what motivated him to buy food for families he's never met." (Does this remind you of anything? Such as our last chapter, when we showed how caring can lead to sharing?)

Kelly said that Greyson's love for Jesus gave him a heart full of compassion for others. She explained the gospel to the man and invited him to church. The man said he'd come, and would bring his son.

The next Sunday, the two of them came to our church. The boy, it turned out, was a special-needs child. This man had no idea that our church has a huge heart for special-needs kids. We have full-time staff, a specialized playground, and classrooms just for these precious children. Over sixty families allow us to care for their children in this ministry every week.

Like a line of dominoes, these events led a family to an encounter with God at our church. The first domino was Greyson asking, "Are we going on a mission trip to Cambodia?" More dominoes toppled as impoverished families in Cambodia were able to eat for a month. The trail of dominoes led to Kelly sharing the gospel with the man at the framing shop, and the man bringing his son to our church. And I'm sure that more dominoes are falling even as you read these words. God's plan is in perpetual motion.

You may take a break, but God never does. He has been working all along, person to person, touch to touch, and what the Spirit moves you to do today is connected, by a long set of "dominoes," from what happened in these chapters of Acts to what you do tomorrow.

Counting Heads and Feeding Hearts

We can't read Acts without noticing the growth spike in the church. Luke gives us the numbers. At Acts 1:15, there were only 120 Christians. At Acts 2:41, three thousand converts were added. By Acts 4:4, the numbers were estimated at five thousand men (meaning as many as twenty thousand men, women, and children).[1] By Acts 5:14, the church had lost count—Luke only tells us that people kept coming.

The explosive growth of the church caused logistical problems for the ministry of caring. Suddenly, according to Acts 6, there was a great influx of widows needing care. As a result, many needy widows in the church were being neglected.

When we grow numerically, we have to be sure we're just as effective in helping people grow spiritually. In other words, we can't separate Acts 2:41 from Acts 2:42. The first verse tells us the church grew in size from 120 to 3,120 in a single day; the next verse tells us these believers were devoted to teaching, fellowship, and prayer. Heads and hearts.

The same challenges come to modern churches. At Houston's First, we make sure we have Christ-centered, Bible-based preaching. But we also realize that the deepest spiritual growth happens away from the worship service, in smaller groups. The souls of believers are more profoundly shaped by discussion and interaction with the Scriptures than by a thirty-minute sermon.

If we focus only on numbers, we won't grow disciples. But as long as we grow disciples, numbers usually follow. A healthy church pursues both kinds of growth.

Every church has a different leadership personality and a different culture. But all churches should have the same focus on Mission 1:8—stepping out into the world to be Christ's witnesses in the power of the Holy Spirit. All churches should seek to be Christ's witnesses locally, nationally, and globally.

In Acts 2:43–47, God gives the early church three areas of focus to keep them on a path of growth, by heads and by hearts: awe of God, unity, and generosity.

In an incredible snapshot of the church at its best, Luke tells us that fear—which simply means a reverent sense of awe—fell across the group, that the apostles began to perform signs and wonders, that "all the believers were together and held all things in common," which simply means unity in the body of Christ, and that "they sold their possessions and property and distributed the proceeds to all, as anyone had need," which simply means they were generous. And in summary,

> Every day they devoted themselves to meeting together in the temple complex, and broke bread from house to house. They ate their food with a joyful and humble attitude, praising God and having favor with all the people. And every day the Lord added to them those who were being saved. (Acts 2:46–47)

Three Signs of Greatness

In three highly critical areas, the church excelled.

1. Awe of God.

What Luke calls *fear* we tend to think of as "awe," that thing you feel when your breath catches, your eyes widen, and you're astounded by what you're seeing. But what caused this? Devotion to the teaching of the apostles. They came to a deeper understanding of the greatness, holiness, and infinite love of God, and they could hardly take it in. They *feared*; they were in awe.

When we're anything less than awestruck by God, something is not right. We're mentally, spiritually, and emotionally off-track. Lack of awe produces shallow devotion; genuine awe produces deep devotion. We should be learning more about God, and knowing Him more deeply every day, and our sense of deep, breathless reverence should only grow stronger, not less so. If you saw the Grand Canyon at sunset every day, the sight might eventually seem nondescript. But wonderful as it is, it's just another created thing. We should never grow accustomed to the majesty of God, never become too jaded to fall on our knees in wonder. Facing the truth about Him, then realizing He loves us and knows every hair on our heads, should move us deeply and profoundly, so that life itself becomes a prayer of praise and worship.

Sadly, many in the church lack awe of the divine. They have it for other things: entertainment, sports teams, wealth, and a thousand other plastic and meaningless items. Whatever profoundly moves us tells a story about what we find "awesome." As a matter of fact, we've done violence to that word by lifting it from the few things it should truly describe and relating it to almost everything else. *This pizza is awesome. That movie is awesome.* When we then say that "our God is an awesome God," we're giving Him the same descriptor we've given these bland and inconsequential things. I wish we could reserve the word *awesome* for Him alone.

2. Unity.

From an awe of God grows a sense of unity. Why is that? It's because of the nature of the church. Distinctions melt away once we agree on the greatness of God and realize that He loves us all, as small as we are. Differences don't really matter because we are brothers and sisters in Christ.

If you have ever seen a disunified church, you know there's nothing less pleasant. A divided church is like a bride fighting with her bridesmaids at the altar, to the embarrassment of the groom. But a unified church—a church characterized by love, caring, compassion, humility, and forgiveness—is one of the most beautiful sights on the planet. A unified church is a gorgeous sight, because it's the bride of Christ in all her radiance, loveliness, and adornment.

3. Generosity.

Unity brings compassion and generosity. When we love one another as we love ourselves, we share accordingly. The awe of God in the unity of the body of Christ produced a lifestyle of amazing generosity in the early church.

We all want to be generous. Why is it such a struggle for us at times? Let me suggest that we tend to forget who owns us.

Proof of Ownership

Every family considers itself a team, and at some point Mom or Dad will say, "Come on, let's work together! Let's show teamwork." Kids will declare their independence, however, by use of the word *mine*.

So you have that family meeting and say, "We're all responsible for keeping the house clean. If you see dirty dishes in the kitchen, towels on the bathroom floor, or clutter in the living room, don't just step over it, clean it up."

And you can predict what's coming. One of the kids will say, "I didn't leave that there, Sis did, and I'm not going to clean it up!"

So you do a word study with your family. You say, "Okay, take out a pen and paper for a vocabulary test. Write down these three phrases: *house payment*, *car payment*, and *utility bill*. Have you ever paid for any of those items? No, you haven't. The money that pays these bills is *mine*. Every bowl of cereal you eat is a gift of parental grace. As your parents, we love you, but we also expect you to be part of the family team. We want to hear less selfishness, more unity, and better service."

Parents who read this are nodding their heads, I'm sure. But isn't that what you and I do with God? Aren't we just as childish and selfish when God asks us to be part of His family team? When He points out a need in our church family, are we quick to set aside some of our personal wants so that we can donate to that need? Or do we clutch our possessions and say "Mine!"?

The moment we say that to God, He says, "Okay, take out a pen and paper, and let's write down a Scripture verse together. Isaiah 66:1—'Heaven is My throne, and earth is My footstool.' What part of My throne did you build? What part of My footstool did you create? Of all the things you say are 'mine,' how much is really yours? And how much is a gift of my grace? You were born on third base, and you think you hit a triple!"

It hurts because it's true. What do we really own? Nothing. God owns it all. Even when we tithe, we only give back 10 percent of the 100 percent God has given to us.

If we are truly in awe of God, generosity will not be a problem for us. We will live a lifestyle of *awe*-some generosity, just like those believers in the early church. It won't even occur to us to hold back anything, because everything belongs to our awesome God.

We're just grateful recipients of His lavish grace.

Watch Your Step!

Mission 1:8 became the heartbeat of the early church, and it grabbed the heart of Houston's First as well. We simply asked everyone in the church to take a step up on his or her generosity. Name of the initiative? You guessed it: Mission 1:8.[2]

Our vision was to plant two multisite campuses in our city and adopt three cities in the nation and three in the world where we would plant churches, while partnering with other ministries to care for the widow, the orphan, the poor, the prisoner, and the refugee. Such an enlarged vision would require much greater generosity on the part of our people, $15 million more than our existing budget over two years.

In leading these initiatives, I've been influenced by Nelson Searcy's book *Maximize*, in which he outlines a "generosity ladder."[3] Here is our church's version of his idea.

Through asking everyone to step up a rung, we saw our missions giving go from 22 percent of our budget to 51 percent! We were even more excited to discover we had 3,800 brand-new givers to God's work, and almost ten thousand families participating. People were coming off the sidelines and getting into the game. Through the generosity of our people, we raised $30 million, twice as much money as we had planned, and were able to make twice the difference.

We helped plant churches in Boston, the Bay Area, New York City, Rio, Madrid, and East Asia. We provided forty-three widows with subsidized income, rescued 195 babies from abortion, translated the New Testament into eleven languages, started two campuses in our city, and partnered with more than thirty ministries. I could go on, but you get the point. Mission 1:8 was fueled by generosity.

Let me make it personal. Kelly and I prayed fervently about what our family's Mission 1:8 commitment should be and the Lord led us to a number that required us to begin tithing twice as much as before. We had been "extravagant givers" for more than a decade, but we knew that increasing our commitment to 20 percent would be a stretch. We took a deep breath, trusted God to provide—and went for the next step.

It's a blessing to be unified in our marriage with regard to giving. I encourage you to pray for that kind of unity and to seek it in your marriage. We saw God provide—and then some. He opened the windows of heaven for us. In two years here's a few examples of what happened:

- Three times we received unexpected money.
- Three times we received for free what we thought we would have to pay for.
- We refinanced our house, lowering our payments by one-third.
- We unknowingly overpaid on our taxes and received twice as much back as we expected.

God blessed us so much that we raised our total amount by 10 percent more after the first year of our two-year commitment. I hope this encourages you to take a step up on the generosity ladder in your life. God doesn't have to respond in your life the same way He did with us. Your adventure will be entirely your own. What I'm saying is this: trust God and take the next step of discipleship and obedience in your giving. Then watch how God uses your increased generosity to make an impact for God's kingdom on the world around you. And watch the impact your giving makes on your own life.

Our blessings were far from just monetary. We had the joy of financial peace instead of stress, and our prayer lives deepened. When lives were changed through Mission 1:8, we knew we had been a part of it.

Even more satisfying, the conversations we had with our kids about sacrifice and service were rich and powerful. Generosity to kingdom purposes is not "Give God a dollar and He'll give you ten." It's "Trust Him with your heart and you'll live a life in the love of God rather than the love of money." God worked in us and in our church, not just through us.

Don't fear the adventure of giving—embrace it. As a friend of mine once said, "Generosity is not something God wants *from* you but *for* you."

Community or Communism?

You might have this question about the ending to Acts 2: Wasn't the early church practicing some form of socialism or communism? I've heard that allegation over the years. After all, the believers had everything in common, they sold their property, and they distributed to anyone who had need. Isn't that what

Karl Marx meant when he said, "From each according to his ability, to each according to his need"?

No, the apostles weren't involved in a program to "redistribute the wealth." They didn't tax the early Christians or force anyone to give up their possessions. Everything came directly from the heart, not by centralized rule. They gave from the overflow of generosity. There's a wide difference between Christian community and Marxist communism.

We need to remember that the book of Acts is descriptive, not prescriptive. In other words, Luke tells us what happened in the early church; it's a history, not a template. There are many situations and actions that Luke describes in Acts (such as casting lots to select a new apostle) that we wouldn't do today.

Then again, it's a wonderful idea to model ourselves and our churches on some of the things we see in Acts. One of these is the extravagant love they practiced. We should study it, marvel at it, and ask how we can imitate it.

Not long after Kelly and I were married, a friend offered me what he called "a surefire investment opportunity." Yes, I gave him the money. And no, I never got a nickel of it back. Money has wings and loves to take flight. But there is one surefire investment opportunity, and that is the kingdom of God. His economy yields great returns—always has and always will. Your investment, however, is through self-sacrificing generosity. And generosity means giving from love rather than duty.

There's how we are, and then there's how we want to be; we want to grow in generosity. So how do we get there? A lot of it has to do with our perspective on these verses in Acts 2. In the past, whenever I read how the early Christians sold their possessions and gave to the poor, I would get a little nervous and uneasy. I would think, *Is it wrong to have a house or car?*

Then one day it hit me: whenever I read those verses, I always identified with the people who sold their possessions. It never occurred to me to identify with the poor. It never occurred to me to read those verses and say, *Let me put myself in the place of someone who hasn't eaten in three days, whose children have no food. It must have been wonderful for them to experience the love and generosity of someone else.*

If you read those verses and identify with the recipient instead of the donor, if you think about what it means to be desperately poor and to receive a material blessing from God's people, it will change your perspective on giving. It certainly changed mine. Empathy is the act of putting yourself in someone's place and feeling what they feel. Once I had vicariously experienced the emotions of someone in need, I wanted to do something about that need. Once I'd vicariously experienced the gratitude of being blessed, I wanted to become a blessing.

If God says give it, you give it. If God says sell it, you sell it. If God says do it, you do it. Giving might become a program at some point, but it begins as an impulse, a desire of the heart. It shouldn't begin as a duty. You should be able to trace a line back in time to your awe before the majesty of God and your feeling of needing to respond in some way. You respond in worship, in unity, and in service to others. You honor God by doing the things He does.

Our problem today isn't that we have too much stuff. It's that we don't have *enough* awe of God.

A Balance to Be Managed

Let me suggest a key principle about giving: *generosity is a balance to be managed, not a problem to be solved.*[4] It is difficult to solve the question of how much we should give, once and for all. It's a tension we must deal with, a balance we must manage throughout our lives.

For example, my son and I have the goal of attending a baseball game in every Major League ballpark by the time he finishes high school. We are well on our way, with over twenty stadiums behind us out of thirty. Each season we pick a couple of ballparks and head out on our "baseball trip." Believe me, flights, hotels, tickets, meals, and souvenirs all add up. Someone could chime in with a, "Just think how that baseball money could have been spent on the needs of the poor."[5]

Well, I do think of those needs. I also think of what my son needs from his dad and the deep conversations we have on our journeys. This is the balance we constantly have to manage: we have to find the balance that's right for our families, budgets, and conscience.

Now, if I took my kids to every single game on the schedule, and if I spent half the family budget on sporting events, we could all agree my balance was way off. But to live with certain tensions is one of life's challenges. Being impact-minded and being a good father are not at odds but rather part of the same whole. Money spent building relationships and creating memories with our children is not a waste but a step of discipleship and love in their lives. Our family goes on mission trips and vacations, both with the desire to share the unstoppable gospel with others.

Finding that balance is tough, especially if we worry more about how other people do it—finding the speck in *their* eye when something bigger may be lodged in our own.

Here are a few questions to ask ourselves:

- How much unused excess do I have? For example, how many rooms in my house are seldom used?
- Could I live with less? In what area am I spending too much? Am I spending borrowed money (debt) or money I have?
- Would my giving be freed up if I got the "better" instead of the "best"?
- Where is my heart in my purchases?
- What if the biggest check I wrote each month was for God's eternal work instead of my house or car?

Please don't hear judgment but rather an invitation to deeper joy. We get it wrong when we think of generosity as a wallet issue. The truth is, it's a discipleship issue. If you take a good, hard look and come to the conclusion that you're not the kind of giver God wants you to be, ask a more foundational question: *Am I the kind of follower of Jesus He wants me to be?*

It's really not rocket science—just give back to God whenever you receive. Start with 2 or 3 percent with a goal of climbing the ladder to 10 percent and beyond. But most of all, take your eyes off the spreadsheet and put them on God. Let yourself be blown away, awestruck by His greatness, and you'll eventually find it's not too difficult to blow past the "extravagant" rung of our ladder.

Put your finances in the right order: give, save, and then spend. Usually we do the opposite. If you take these steps, you will find God faithful, I assure you. And you'll see lives changed and needs met through your generosity.

Christians are often hesitant to talk about money—to put it mildly. If we were just talking about money, I wouldn't blame them. But this is a chapter—and a topic—about deep, abiding reverence for God and how it affects us. Don't strain to give; strain to be more in God's presence, to experience more of Him in your life, and the giving will flow naturally from your life. *If we live in awe of God, we will let Him do whatever He wants through us, and there is no limit to what He can accomplish.*

The church in Acts 2 taught about God, rediscovered an awe for Him, found themselves more in unity, and then found themselves giving without restraint. How do you think that affected the community around them? People wanted in, and fast. They wanted that kind of love, that kind of joy. And the church grew, explosively and powerfully, without anyone running a program or coming up with a gimmick. People wanted God, and now they could see where to find Him. All because a small group of believers were in awe before their Lord.

Aristides the Athenian was a second-century Greek writer best known for a book called *The Apology of Aristides*. In that book, he describes the lifestyle of the early Christians:

> They know and believe in God, the Maker of heaven and earth, in whom are all things and from whom are all things. . . . They walk in all humility and kindness, and falsehood is not found among them, and they love one another: and from the widows they do not turn away their countenance: and they rescue the orphan from him who does him violence: and he who has gives to him who has not, without grudging. . . .
>
> And if there is among them a man that is poor or needy, and they have not an abundance of necessaries, they fast two or three days that they may supply the needy with their necessary food.[6]

I can't read that without being profoundly moved. This is a Greek writer describing the adherents of this new belief system in which falsehood is not to be found, in which hurting people are comforted, in which kindness rules, and in which people would rather go hungry themselves than see anyone else miss a meal.

And it's funny how that works. What happens when people begin to fast? They experience a deeper spirituality, which means they draw near to God and feel a sense of awe. And then they're unified even more—and you can fill in the rest. It's another cycle, another round of seasons that God has designed. Winter to spring, caring to sharing, unity to generosity.

A staff member told me that he went on a mission trip to a poor country with the intention of ministering to the spiritual and physical needs of the people there. The believers in that country had very little, yet they fasted for several days so that they would have food to share with the American missionaries.

When you see that brand of generosity, it means God's Spirit is in the room and people are feeling a sense of awe for their Creator. May we be unified by reverence for Him and the joy of giving, one to another.

7

At the Corner of Now and Eternity

How Life Happens at Intersections

My local car wash has a popcorn machine and a shoeshine stand. All my love languages meet efficiently in one place: a snack, a clean car, and shined shoes! Once I went to the shoeshine stand, and the man who shines shoes was sitting reading his Bible. I said, "Hey, that's a good book!"

He said, "It certainly is."

We chatted, and I learned that he was the pastor of a small Hispanic church. Because the church couldn't afford to pay him full-time, he was shining shoes on the side. I could see the joy radiating from his face when he talked to me. He gave each of his customers a very enthusiastic shoeshine because he was shining shoes in the name of Jesus.

He told me of a time when another one of his regular customers walked up as he was shining shoes and said good-naturedly, "Hey, why aren't you reading your Bible?"

"Well," my new friend said, "there's a time to *read* your Bible—and there's a time to *do* your Bible."

In Acts 2, Peter preached from the Bible. Now, in Acts 3, we'll see the apostles Peter and John not merely reading and preaching the Bible—they're going to *do* the Bible. And they're going to provoke a crisis.

Intersection Brings Opportunity

As Acts 3 opens, Peter and John go up to the temple in Jerusalem to pray and to preach Christ. They are still practicing Jews but their faith has been completed by the work of Christ.

As they approach the temple gate, they see a disabled man being placed there by others so he could beg for donations from those who passed. It's similar to a scene we might see in urban America; people walk on, avoiding eye contact. Not Peter and John. They make eye contact and say, "Look at us."

The beggar does so, hoping for a few nice coins.

Peter says, "I don't have silver or gold, but what I have, I give you: In the name of Jesus Christ the Nazarene, get up and walk!" (Acts 3:6). He then takes the disabled man by the right hand and pulls him to his feet. The man, of course, expects to topple to the ground immediately. Yet his feet and ankles now support him perfectly.

Later in the passage, we find that this man is more than forty years old and has been lame since birth (4:22). Think of the wild emotional ride the disabled man experienced: disappointment at being told there's no money, terror at being yanked to his feet, and incredulous joy when he is suddenly healed.

The man, of course, begins a euphoric celebration in the most public spot in the whole country. Everyone sees him leaping, kicking his heels, laughing, and praising God at the top of his lungs. This is a man who has become a public landmark on the walk to the temple, as much a fixture as the gate itself. No one has ever seen him stand, and now they see him dance.

There's a powerful lesson here in *the importance of being aware of the individual.* Peter and John have just seen three thousand people come to Christ in one day. Peter has just preached the first sermon in church history. High times indeed. But their heads are not in the clouds; their feet are still planted solidly on the ground. And they do just what Jesus did—look at individuals as if, at that moment, no one else matters.

Peter and John could be thinking big about now—at three thousand heads per day, how long before they're running this nation? They could be figuring people might have to buy a ticket to hear from them after today. But these two, who in more immature days argued about who would be greatest in the kingdom of God, have their pride at bay. They want to go to the ends of the earth for Christ but they're not going to lose sight of who is right in their path.

They learned this principle while walking with Jesus. He preached to the crowds, then interacted with individuals. One was no more important than the other.

The principle that emerges from this account is this: *intersection brings opportunity.*

Whenever you get in your car and drive any distance at all, you pass intersection after intersection—crossroads with crosswalks and stop lights and stop signs. That's a picture of everyday life, which is made of intersections and crossings. As your path brings you to an interaction with another individual at work or in the neighborhood, that's one more intersection. Stop, look, and listen!

Too often we drive on through without taking in the sights. If you do that, you miss the point of living. God put us on this pathway to impact and influence lives along our journey. We need to be aware of the people coming and going from the moments of our lives.

It's been said that life is what happens while we're making other plans. The problem with divine intersections is that we're usually heading somewhere else. These crossings don't fit our schedule or our agenda.

Not every encounter is a divine intersection—if it were, we'd never arrive anywhere! But there are more of them than we perceive. God brings people into our lives for a reason. He wants us to slow down and to allow ourselves to be divinely inconvenienced for the sake of the unstoppable gospel, and for the sake of the individual.

By nature, we don't like red lights and stop signs but we need to realize how often they're more than interruptions to the journey—they are the journey itself. When ministry opportunities arise, we need to be ready to stop and render assistance in the name of Jesus. There is never a wrong time to encourage or help someone.

Peter and John were heading for the temple but their main business was at the temple gate. How often do we walk by people and needs that were placed before us for a reason? How often have we stepped on the gas rather than opening our eyes to see the opportunity before us? God's work might be sitting at the gate instead of at our perceived destination.

I Brake for God Moments

I attended Southwestern Baptist Theological Seminary, Houston extension, then on the campus of Houston Baptist University. HBU is a Christian university that nonetheless has some non-believing students.

One week I was in the student union, studying for a huge theology test. I wore a T-shirt emblazoned with the theme of a student retreat where I'd spoken. The shirt said, "Six Hours One Friday," referring to the hours of Jesus on the cross.

Someone walked up. "Can I ask you a question?"

I had a huge test in thirty minutes—so, no, I didn't need a Q&A session. But I looked at him and politely said, "Sure."

"What does 'Six Hours One Friday' mean?"

And of course I recognized the intersection.

I prayed, *Lord, what should I do?* It was a comical enigma: Was I going to be a Pharisee studying theology, or an Acts-style Christian with a hungry soul? The answer was clear. We discussed the meaning of the cross. But on the inside, I was saying, *This is important, Lord, but do You think You could save him in the next five minutes? I still need to cram.*

But it didn't play out that way. This young man had some heavy questions, and after thirty minutes, he finally accepted Christ. I got his phone number, promised to follow up, and made a mad dash for class. Somehow the test hadn't begun, though I was late. I shared my experience with the class and led everyone in prayer for my new friend.

Then I asked the prof, "Is there extra credit for leading a guy to Christ before a theology exam?" I was joking. Sort of. The prof laughed. "No. You're saved by grace, but you graduate by works."

I could have stepped on the gas and said, "No time, friend—in a hurry!" when he asked about my shirt. I had a stark choice between studying the Bible or doing it, and this was a moment for doing it. I know I haven't always made the right choice, but that was a day when I did.

We need to brake for God moments. Sometimes we don't do it because we don't think we're worthy or ready to share the gospel.

Notice that Peter and John had no silver or gold. But they saw the opportunity. Sometimes we step on the gas because we think we lack resources. *I don't have the words. I don't have the doctrine. I don't have anything to offer this person.* You always have what you need to do God's work; otherwise He wouldn't have brought you to this intersection. Peter and John offered the disclaimer. They said, "We don't have any money, but we have something else to offer you." They had Jesus, and He is always enough. You have Him too. What else do you need?

An Irrelevant in the Room

What a spectacle this man must have been, taking his new feet for a test drive. He may have run a full lap around the temple, because he met Peter and John again at Solomon's Colonnade, and he grabbed himself a handful of disciples. By this time, quite a crowd was gathering. And what did Peter see? A major intersection.

Peter decided it was time to preach the second sermon in church history. He asked the people why they were so amazed. Did they think the disciples healed by their own power? And he brought the discussion right back to Jesus, the man many of them had cursed when He was in the hands of the Romans. Peter said, "By faith in His name, His name has made this man strong, whom you see and know. So the faith that comes through Him has given him this perfect health in front of all of you" (Acts 3:16).

Again, we can't help but notice the humility. Peter has become a persuasive preacher. He and John have just done the kind of miracle that Jesus did. Do you think you or I might be a little cocky in these circumstances? Peter could have been a rock star. Instead, he was quick to point to the One whose power they'd actually seen.

We all know false humility when we hear it—and we're not hearing it from Peter. He knows by now that he is nothing without Jesus Christ, and he is quick to give Him the glory.

Notice the *boldness* here too. Peter doesn't tailor the truth—he says what needs to be said. This crowd has rejected Jesus and had Him crucified, and there's no use letting it be the elephant in the room. Crowds don't like accusatory statements, and they might well have turned into a mob. They'd certainly done it before. But Peter has trusted in Christ for a healing, and now he trusts Him again.

Throughout Acts we notice how the early church hits the truth right on the nose. These men shared Jesus without ifs, ands, buts, or regard for convenience or political correctness. They also stayed relevant to the issues of the day.

People don't seem to think the church is very relevant these days. If they really believed it was, we'd have traffic jams on every road leading to a steeple. There are traffic jams for rush hour, because work is relevant. There's congestion leaving town on a holiday weekend, because vacations are relevant. Sporting events? People are willing to sit in traffic for many hours, because entertainment is relevant. People believe all these things speak to what's important to them—but somehow the church doesn't have anything important to say.

We, the church leaders, know this, and to our detriment some of us have tried to be more "relevant" by de-emphasizing the inconvenient aspects of the gospel. We hide the cross and share only the aspects of Jesus that we think will be attractive. That's why we need to study the sermons of the first-century church. If we place Jesus—all of Jesus—front and center, preach the cross, and insist on the Lordship of Christ, people will realize the relevance. They will say, "There's nothing in the world more important to my life than this message I'm hearing."

Cross-less Christianity and happy-talk sermons? Those are truly irrelevant.

The Mirror Never Lies

Peter stood at the intersection of Judaism and Christianity, the intersection of the Old Testament and the New, the intersection of BC and AD, and he spoke boldly. Would the crowd respond with repentance—or rage?

As Peter addressed this Jewish crowd, he identified with them, calling them "fellow Israelites." He quoted the words of Moses, who had prophesied to Israel that God would raise up a Messiah from among the people. He cited all the prophets from Samuel onward, who foretold the coming of the Messiah. He reminded them of the promise God made to Abraham, "Through your offspring all peoples on earth will be blessed."

Peter drew a line from Hebrew to Christian. The prophecy that must have come to mind for the audience was Isaiah 53, which describes the Messiah as a suffering servant. What must it have been like to suddenly make that connection, and realize that you yourself helped cause the suffering?

Isaiah had written, "He was pierced because of our transgressions" (53:5) and they thought of the nails. He'd written that the Deliverer would be "crushed because of our iniquities" (v. 5) and they recalled the crown of thorns. "He was oppressed and afflicted," read the prophecy, "yet He did not open His mouth" (v. 7). And they knew that indeed, Jesus had kept His silence before Pilate. Most of these people would have memorized those words—then they lived them.

The whole story of Jesus, from nativity to Calvary, had been written in the Scriptures that made up the sacred backdrop to these people's lives. Now Peter was brazen enough to show them the shocking truth—how they had played out the villain's role in their ultimate story of hope—and he demanded repentance for the promise of grace and forgiveness.

We're part of a living story too. The Christian faith is not a mere two thousand years old. It stretches back to the book of Genesis, when the first two people sinned, and when God promised them that a Savior would come. And as a symbol of the sacrificial death of the Savior, God sacrificed an animal and clothed the man and the woman in its skin.

Our faith is rooted in the signs and prophecies that begin in the early pages of Genesis and continue throughout the books of Moses, the prophets, the Psalms, and on into the books of the New Testament. If Peter's audience looked into his teaching like a mirror, so do we. It convicts us, demands repentance—and gives us hope.

In 2012, a seventy-five-year-old woman named Marion Shurtleff purchased a Bible in a used bookstore in California. She got home, began to flip through the pages, and came across two sheets of paper folded and tucked into the middle. With natural curiosity, she unfolded the yellowing notebook paper and saw her own name. With a gasp, she came to realize that here was an essay she'd written in an effort to earn a Girl Scout merit badge in Kentucky—two thousand miles and sixty-five years ago. That forgotten essay had worked itself across time and space to speak to her as an elderly woman.[1]

When we look into the Bible, we look into ourselves. This book recognizes no boundaries of time or geography. It speaks truth into every life, and it can do that only because it is the Word of God, and it stands forever. If we can trust God's Word deeply, then we can trust God Himself. God, who strengthened the feet and ankles of the disabled man, hasn't run short of power. The message is still true, the miracles still come, and the implications are as relevant as the next breath you take.

Your Face in the Crowd

The busiest and most dangerous intersection of all is the moment of decision. Peter reminds the people that they've made a wrong turn. "But you denied the Holy and Righteous One," he told them, "and asked to have a murderer given to you. You killed the source of life, whom God raised from the dead; we are witnesses of this" (Acts 3:14–15).

In witnessing for Jesus, Peter is also witness to the evil behavior he saw when Jesus was handed over to His executioners. And just as the disciple points his finger at the crowd, he also points toward you and me. Would we have done any better than those people did? Would we have refused to take a bite out of the apple offered in Eden? God knows our hearts, and we do too. Again, we look into the Word of Life and see ourselves, blemishes and all.

I think back to my first sixteen years of life and have a pretty good idea where that young man was heading. By the grace of God, I met Christ that year. But every single day, I must make the decision to let Christ live through me. The "old man" is defeated—but he still shows up to deceive (see Rom. 6:5–11; Eph. 4:22–24).

Peter addressed people who had chosen Barabbas to go free and Jesus to die. They had come to the intersection of a murderer and the perfect Son of God, and taken the worst road imaginable. And before we in turn condemn them, we must ask: How often do we, too, choose convenience over conviction, money over meaning, abortion over adoption, selfishness over significance, or gratification over God?

I would like to feel superior to that mob, but my sins put Jesus on the cross no less than theirs. I must say I can see myself in that crowd, crying "Give us Barabbas!" How about you?

Even so, let's not forget the unstoppable gospel offered to us. We made the decision to crucify, but God made the decision to resurrect. We made the decision to rebel, but God made the decision of grace. We bear the taint of death, but Christ is the source of our life. Is He yours?

If we played a quick word game, and you had to answer quickly, how would you fill in this blank?

"I am a _____."

It's one thing to answer thoughtfully while reading a Christian book—but how would you answer in the middle of the day, caught up in life, without time to process it? In your heart, how do you choose to identify yourself?

I am a mom.

I am a dad.

I am a student.

I am a salesman.
I am a conservative.
I am a liberal.
I am a fan of my team.

Your source of life will come through in your answer. What or who defines you? If you're a true follower of Jesus Christ, your blank would reflect it by saying *Christian* or *follower of Christ* or *child of the King.* Everything else is just details.

In our culture, occupations become our descriptors. "Hi, my name is Gregg Matte and I am a pastor." But I don't see myself that way primarily, nor as a husband or a father. I am a follower of Jesus Christ. Being a pastor, a husband, and a father—these things are precious to me, but only one thing ultimately reveals my source of life. My earthly roles are trumped and actually empowered by my heavenly identity.

Peter says, "You killed the source of life. . . . Therefore repent and turn back, so that your sins may be wiped out, that seasons of refreshing may come from the presence of the Lord, and that He may send Jesus, who has been appointed for you as the Messiah" (Acts 3:15, 19–20). They—and we—have made too many wrong turns. Now there's only one route remaining, and it leads to forgiveness, peace, salvation, joy, and eternity.

Across the world, this very moment, countless people sit at that intersection—watching the traffic light. Deep in their souls they sense it's a time for turning. There's a decision to make, and they also know that it's no cheap or easy decision. It will be Jesus or Barabbas, heaven or hell, the prison of the moment or the limitlessness of eternity. I wonder if you're sitting at that intersection right this second. I wonder which friends of yours need you to be Peter and to point the way.

Or maybe it's another kind of moment—a person whose life has intersected with yours, a difference you could make, maybe even something you *shouldn't* do. Maybe this intersection is about grace and patience only.

Whatever the case, your moment's greatest enemy is *hurry*. Don't we do enough hurrying? Does it ever really lead to anything good—or just to stress and wasted moments? Please don't hurry. Please don't be distracted. Look this moment in the eye and listen to your soul. What is Christ calling on you to do? How can you serve Him? What possibilities might life hold if, this one time, you slowed down rather than stepping on the gas, and became a servant of God in this moment?

These intersections are not places to sit in impatience. They are where life happens. They're not interruptions of the journey—they *are* the journey. Wherever you're heading may be of no significance at all, but where you are right now is the place where God has put you. It's a place that touches eternity. Intersections are where the *people* are; where the *needs* are.

And have you noticed? If you look from above, intersections make the shape of the cross.

8

Courageous
at the Flashpoint

Showing Grace under Fire

Hitler called the leaders of the German church to his office in 1934. He wanted them to know that they'd better start supporting his programs. A pastor named Martin Niemöller explained that he had to be faithful to the gospel.

That night the Gestapo raided his home. Then a bomb exploded in his church. The secret police continued to harass him, yet Niemoller preached, "We must obey God rather than man." Soon he was arrested and placed in solitary confinement. As they led him toward an underground chamber in 1938, he almost gave in to his fear. The guard pushed him along at gunpoint. But as they came to the final flight of stairs, there was a whispering sound—so soft it could almost be missed. He realized he was hearing Proverbs 18:10: "The name of Yahweh is a strong tower; the righteous run to it and are protected." It was the voice of the guard, just behind him.

Niemoller felt new strength, and he clung to that verse through his trial, and after that, years in concentration camps until the war ended in 1945.[1]

We all want to be obedient to God, but what happens when that gets us in trouble? Where will the courage come from then? As we've seen, Peter and John had healed a disabled man in the name of Christ. It caused a commotion—and trouble for Peter and John.

As Acts 4 opens, these disciples are arrested in the midst of a sermon. Darkness is falling at the end of the day, but a new light is breaking for many who were in the crowd: "But many of those who heard the message believed, and the number of the men came to about 5,000" (Acts 4:4).

Here we see the first confrontation between the early Christian church and the forces of persecution. Up to this point, the church has made a favorable impression on the community. Acts 2:47 tells us they enjoyed the "favor of all the people."

It's no longer *all* the people. The church is about to find itself at odds with the power structure in Jerusalem, as Peter and John are hauled away, under arrest.

Profiles in Courage

Fort Sumter was the flashpoint of the American Civil War. Pearl Harbor was the flashpoint of America's entrance to World War II. And 9/11 was the flashpoint of the War on Terror. Here in Acts 4, we see the flashpoint of the war between the church and the forces of persecution. This war still rages today. After twenty centuries, Christians are still told, "Don't speak about Jesus."

The only problem for those authorities is that this is a new Peter. In Luke 22:54–62, three different people identified Peter as one of the followers of Jesus—and each time, Peter denied knowing Jesus, though he had promised his Master, "Lord, I am ready to go with you to prison and to death."

Now, in Acts 4, Peter gets a do-over. He has an opportunity to demonstrate the courage that failed him in the hours before the crucifixion. In fact, he has a chance to demonstrate that courage in front of the very same people who terrified him before.

Peter the Petrified now becomes Peter the Passionate, the Fearless.

So the question that confronts you and me in Acts 4 is this: Do we want to be people of courage? Do you want to be known as a man or woman of courage in your family, in your workplace, in your church, in your community, and in your nation? Do you want to be known as a person who stands firmly in the midst of turbulent times? Do you want to be known as a person who declares Jesus to be the Way, the Truth, and the Life, no matter what the cost? Of course you do.

In Harper Lee's *To Kill a Mockingbird*, the hero, Atticus Finch, says to his son, Jem, "I wanted you to see what real courage is, instead of getting the idea that courage is a man with a gun in his hand. It's when you know you're licked before you begin, but you begin anyway, and you see it through no matter what."[2]

That's the thing. Courage is no guarantee of victory—that's what makes it courageous! Standing tall in the face of sure defeat marks real bravery. It's sharing Christ when you know there's a cost. Mission 1:8 demands people like that.

The irony is that courage actually requires fear. It's not the absence of fear but the mastery of it. You stand by your principles rather than your emotions. You do what you've determined is right rather than listening to those screaming, "Turn back!"

Courage is only manifest in confrontation. The confrontation may be between you and another person, or between you and a dangerous situation, or between you and your hidden insecurities and irrational fears, but fear is always part of the itinerary. There are no detours around it. If you never face a confrontation, if you never face your fear, how will you know if you have courage?

Courage is like a diamond on black velvet. It shines the brightest against the darkest of circumstances. If a running back scores a touchdown when there's no defense on the field, does he deserve praise for the touchdown? No. Courage always involves confrontation and the strong possibility of suffering. The greater the opposition, the greater the courage.

Peter and John watched a mob carry Jesus away, beat Him, hammer nails through Him, and leave Him to die slowly and cruelly. This isn't a theoretical idea—they'd seen crucifixions. Everyone in Jerusalem had. Now they're looking into the eyes of that same mob. There has been no warning, no time to pray for strength. The crisis moment just springs upon them.

There is one thing in their favor: they're riding the spiritual victory of five thousand new believers. Peter and John know that God is on the job.

They also know the three groups named by Luke—priests, Sadducees, and temple police—who make up the mob. The priests are essentially the bureaucrats in charge of operating the temple. The captain of the temple guard is the temple's chief of police. And the Sadducees are a socially and politically powerful sect in Judean society. We know they didn't believe in any kind of afterlife, and Luke tells us they were upset by all the resurrection talk. When people are out in public disproving your entire worldview, you become angry.

Morning comes, and in Acts 4:5–7 Peter and John are brought to stand trial before Annas the high priest, his son-in-law Caiaphas (a ringleader of the plot against Jesus), plus other members of the high priest's family. All of these people figured in the trial and execution of Jesus.

So Peter and John know the score. These are corrupt and hateful officials, not above bringing in false witnesses. It will be an easy matter to trump up charges that Peter and John are inciting rebellion. Then it's a short path up that same hill where Jesus was led. And if it happened to Jesus Himself, why not two of His disciples?

That's what Peter and John are facing. It's a moment to be courageous—or not.

Prison a Privilege?

Two months ago, Peter lost his composure and denied his Lord in a setting much less threatening than this one. But we're going to see a very different man, and we have to ask ourselves why. What accounts for the change?

Acts 1:8 does: "But you will receive power when the Holy Spirit has come on you."

That's the same Holy Spirit you've received if you're a follower of Jesus Christ. Think about that as you mull over the things that frighten you.

The Sanhedrin was an assembly of twenty-three elders, and every city in Israel had one. But, with all its power, this council sat and watched as people came to Christ by the thousands. Peter and John could have focused on that intimidating group of twenty-three men, forgetting that thousands of others had their backs. I've had moments when one angry email has threatened to overshadow all those who were praying for me, all those who supported me, and of course the Holy Spirit Himself. Times of conflict and confrontation can make us lose our perspective.

We can also lose sight of the fact that one fully committed believer plus God is a majority in any situation. When we face opposition, we will find our courage if we listen to the voice of God, not the voice of men. There will always be those who say it can't be done; we have to be the people who say, "I am able to do all things through Him who strengthens me" (Phil. 4:13).

I don't want to minimize the crisis Peter and John faced. Their opponents wanted nothing more than to find some pretext by which to put these two men to death. In Acts 7, many of these same men will take part in the stoning of Stephen, the first Christian martyr. So there's murderous intent simmering below the surface of the trial of Peter and John.

Yet I believe it was a genuine honor for these two pioneers of the faith to be the first persons jailed for the sake of the gospel. No one wants imprisonment. But receiving it for the sake of Jesus and His gospel would cause us to look back with honor some later day. As Jesus said, "Those who are persecuted for righteousness are blessed, for the kingdom of heaven is theirs" (Matt. 5:10).

This does not mean that we are holy masochists who want to bring persecution down on our heads. But we know what happens when the church is attacked: faith grows. God moves. We grow bolder when our courage is put to the test, and we remember that the gospel is unstoppable.

Getting in the Spirit

The members of the Sanhedrin interrogated Peter and John about the healing of the disabled man: "By what power or in what name have you done this?" (Acts 4:7). Peter must be thinking, *I'm glad you asked that question!*

Luke tells us that Peter is "filled with the Holy Spirit" at this moment. The Spirit always supplies courage. When you sense an opening to share Christ, don't back down. Ask for the filling of the Holy Spirit, then speak boldly. If your college professor mocks the Christian faith, be filled by the Spirit, then speak respectfully but boldly.

We need to clarify our thinking. We are baptized with the Spirit—once and for all—on the moment of conversion. There's never a need to ask for it again, because it's accomplished. But we need to ask to be *filled* with the Holy Spirit regularly (see Acts 9:17, Eph. 5:18). What does that mean? We make ourselves available to God. We say, "Fill me, use me, and speak through me." The Spirit is always present, but when we offer ourselves completely to His desires for us, in those moments we find that we have His words, His courage, and His understanding of a situation. We're able to do as Jesus would do.

If you don't find yourself talking about Jesus, you're probably not yielding to the Holy Spirit. When you're cooperating freely and intentionally with Him, you have an unstoppable passion for sharing Christ, for ministering to others, and for being a servant of Christ above all things. This is what Peter lacked when he denied Jesus, and what he has now.

This disciple speaks boldly and eloquently. He says it right out: the disabled man was healed in the name of Jesus Christ "whom you crucified and whom God raised from the dead" (v. 10). If you're worried about a fire that is beginning to rage nearby, do you pour on a little gasoline? That's what Peter does when he not only acknowledges their hand in the crucifixion but also points out that God foiled their efforts by raising Jesus from the dead.

I can imagine Him looking Annas and Caiaphas in the eye as he says, "whom you crucified," and at the Sadducees, who believed death was final, when he said, "whom God raised from the dead." It's equal opportunity provocation.

He does something else I find interesting. He refers to Psalm 118:22, about the stone rejected by the builders becoming a cornerstone—but he makes it "the stone rejected by *you* builders" (Acts 4:11). This is cherished Scripture to those on the council, and Peter turns it against them. He's telling them they executed their own Messiah, after waiting for Him all their lives, and their parents and their parents before them had also waited for Him. Peter could say nothing more incendiary, more offensive.

Then, lest you think he's speaking to nobody but long-dead Hebrew leaders, he throws in a statement that would offend many in our own time: "There is salvation in no one else, for there is no other name under heaven given to people, and we must be saved by it" (v. 12). People today would like to make a mishmash of religions—to place them on a great worldview smorgasbord and let us take what we like from each one. Christianity isn't part of a balanced religious "meal," it's the whole meal. Peter tells us here there is one way to heaven.

It's courageous for Peter to tell the Sanhedrin they've executed their only hope of salvation, that they've wrapped their lives around a religion that is ultimately useless without Jesus. Peter of the three denials has come quite a long way—so why not us?

I would like to have that kind of boldness. Wouldn't you? I've prayed for courage and received it on a number of occasions. I've come to a point where I become weary of my own anxiety and terror and simply lay it before God. It's amazing what happens when we do that. The whole world changes right before our eyes. We see that nothing is impossible through Him—and nothing worthwhile is possible without Him.

In verse 13, we're told that the leaders see exactly what we see in Peter and John. They're "amazed," and they "recognized that they had been with Jesus." When people think of us as Christians, they know where the change comes from and God gets the glory. Time spent with Jesus builds courage. The leaders see the character of Jesus etched into the faces of these former fishermen.

And it doesn't help that the formerly disabled man is now *standing* in their presence. There isn't any opening to say that the disciples are full of hot air, not when they've put this well-known beggar on his feet for the first time. And Luke tells us "they had nothing to say in response" (v. 14).

Nothing to say. Let's look at that one a little closer. If they can't say anything about the disabled man because everyone knows he's no longer disabled—what does that say about Peter's claims of Jesus's resurrection? It tells us they can't argue because everyone in the room knows it happened. Otherwise, surely Caiaphas or Annas would have snapped, "The body of Jesus is in that tomb and we all know it!"

Their silence tells us all we need to know about the evidence for the resurrection.

Crowd Pleasers and God Pleasers

So the council is realizing this isn't going to end well. They have Peter and John taken away, and a debate ensues.

This is the conversation I imagine:

"What do we do now?"

"I say we send them up for insurrection—crucify them!"

"Have you lost your mind? Everybody in Jerusalem knows they healed that man. People are giving glory to God. Do you want the mob to turn on us?"

"He's right—we thought we'd solved the Jesus problem, and we only made things worse. Kill two of them, it could be twice the problem. We'll make martyrs of them."

"Well, we have to shut them up somehow. They're gaining followers by the minute."

There is shouting and bickering, and finally they throw up their hands and let Peter and John off with a stern warning. The disciples, still full of courage, ask their accusers to decide who they should listen to: God or a committee. And they add, "We are *unable to stop* speaking about what we have seen and heard" (vv. 19–20, emphasis added).

It's all about pleasing God instead of people. We all want to please others, and we should. "Each one of us must please his neighbor for his good, to build him up" (Rom. 15:2). The problem comes when we seek our validation from others instead of God. Is it really someone else's approval that counts most? Of course not.

I can be the "chief of sinners" on this one. Like everyone else, I want to be loved. But I won't compromise the gospel to earn another slice of that love.

All too often, we are like a sign I once read: "I'm a recovering people pleaser—is that okay?" A healthy Christian outlook is, "I don't minister to be validated. I minister because I *am* validated. I don't minister to be approved. I minister because I *am* approved. I don't minister because I'm insecure. I minister because I'm *so* secure."

If you're a people pleaser, think hard about Peter and John, who offended everyone in the room when the name of Jesus was at stake—and when everyone in the room had the power to have them killed. Peter could say, as Paul later would: "For am I now trying to win the favor of people, or God? Or am I striving to please people? If I were still trying to please people, I would not be a slave of Christ" (Gal. 1:10).

Peter and John didn't just talk Jesus—they walked Him, showing His power, so that their accusers were afraid to take action. That's courage.

People are still afraid to talk Jesus. They'll say the name of God in an abstract way. They'll be vaguely "spiritual." But the name of Jesus is trouble. Why? Because it carries power. It threatens the power structures of this world; it did so in the first century and still does in the twenty-first.

The high priest Annas and his son-in-law Caiaphas had been installed by the oppressive Roman government as instruments to keep the peace in the conquered Judean province. A popular uprising might get Annas and Caiaphas removed from power. Yes, their beliefs were being challenged, but it was the challenge of power that got their attention. Isn't it interesting that the two fishermen who seemed powerless spoke in courage and power? The two men who had the Romans behind them—the world's greatest empire—were living in fear. They couldn't control the authorities, they couldn't control God, and they couldn't control anyone capable of getting a disabled man back on his feet.

People oppose the name of Jesus because they fear the power of God.

Suppressing or Confessing the Name

Yes, the movers and shakers were shaking with fear. They knew a miraculous healing could come only from God. Had heaven turned against them?

The religious leaders were frightened because they had heard from God. Yet hearing from God is a blessing. When we reach a place in which we don't want to hear from God, that ought to tell us we're in the wrong neighborhood. God always wants what's best for us, and we also know that if we rely on no one but ourselves, it's going to catch up with us sooner or later.

So what was logical for the religious leaders? I would imagine their conversation would go this way:

"You know what? Jesus did some amazing things. Now His followers are doing them."

"I'm thinking the same thing. It might be time for me to reexamine my beliefs."

"Me too. I mean, God is in control—we all know that. And miracles point to God. So what does it say about us if we're on the other side?"

"Let's call those two fishermen back in and find out where we can sign up."

That, of course, would have made perfect sense. It was time to rejoice that the Messiah had come, and to embrace Him and obey Him. Instead, they called Peter and John back and said, "*Shhhh!* Just keep it to yourself in the future."

And it's still happening:

- In May 2011, a federal judge threatened jail time—yes, *jail time*—for student valedictorians in a Texas school district if they led a commencement ceremony in prayer or even mentioned "a supreme being" in a commencement speech. The ruling was reversed on appeal.[3]
- In the spring of 2010, folks at a senior citizens center in Port Wentworth, Georgia, were told they could no longer

pray before meals because the food they were praying over was partially subsidized by the federal government.[4]

- In Minnesota, Florida, Massachusetts, and elsewhere, senior citizens living in federally subsidized housing projects have been told they cannot discuss the Bible, sing Christmas carols, or even display Christmas decorations on the doors of their private apartments. These policies have been reversed, but only after legal pressure from religious freedom organizations.[5]

- Department of Veterans Affairs officials at the Houston National Cemetery have banned the words "God" and "Jesus" from funeral services for military veterans, and have required that prayers be submitted in advance for approval. These restrictions were still being enforced even after a federal judge ordered them stopped.[6]

- In 2005, a federal district judge, in a case called Hinrichs v. Bosma, ordered the Indiana House of Representatives to stop opening with "sectarian" prayers. The judge defined "sectarian prayers" as prayers offered in the name of Jesus. A prayer offered by a Muslim imam in the name of Allah, however, was permissible under the ruling.[7]

- In my hometown of Houston, five pastors received subpoenas for their sermons to be turned in to our city government for review. Only after tremendous pressure from Christians and even non-Christians in Houston and around the nation did the City of Houston withdraw the subpoenas.[8]

Forces in our culture want to erase the name of Jesus from the public square. This is spiritual warfare, as Paul describes in Ephesians 6:12: "For our battle is not against flesh and blood, but against the rulers, against the authorities, against the world

129

powers of this darkness, against the spiritual forces of evil in the heavens."

It takes courage to fight a spiritual war. We have to rise up with courage and say, "No, the name of Jesus is nonnegotiable." If we lose our voice, we lose our impact.

I'm not saying we should be obnoxious about the name of Jesus. The name of this book isn't *Arrogant Gospel* or *Annoying Gospel*. We should love the atheist and non-Christian well. We should be humble and respectful, patterning ourselves after our Lord. But people in power seem to forget the "freedom" clauses in the First Amendment—freedom of speech, freedom of religion. We as believers need to remember high school valedictorians, senior citizens, chaplains, and all the rest of us have a constitutionally protected right to name the name of Jesus.

That name is powerful. There is no other name under which anyone can be saved. Remove the name of Jesus, and you deprive the world of salvation and leave humanity to its own futility. Jesus said "I am the way, the truth, and the life. No one comes to the Father except through Me" (John 14:6).

They Had Been with Jesus

Fearful leaders encountered bold disciples, and all they could do was ask them to stop talking. Luke tells us that the leaders, on encountering Peter and John, "were amazed and recognized that they had been with Jesus" (Acts 4:13).

The leaders were powerful, refined, educated men who knew they were encountering powerless, blue-collar fishermen—and were intimidated by them. They had seen this story before, and the piercing eyes of Jesus were shining through those of the fishermen. The wisdom of Jesus echoed in their words.

The courage of Jesus blazed in their eyes. They had been with Jesus, and it showed.

We use all kinds of strategies to impress people—to go to church or to do anything else. But here's the message: people will be impressed when they see we've been with Jesus.

You can't do that by proximity. There isn't a mountain to climb. Going to the Holy Land won't get you any closer to Jesus. Your proximity to the Father, the Son, and the Holy Spirit never changes. You're as close to Him right now as you'll ever be.

No, it's about *intimacy* rather than proximity. That's something you can change. Jesus is with you every moment, but are you with Him? Sometimes we feel the tug at our hearts to speak His name, to be closer to Him, and we tell ourselves, *Shhhh!* We suppress it, and what a tragedy that is. We can be experiencing deep fellowship and love anytime we wish. We can be coming before Him in prayer, experiencing Him through His Word, exalting Him in worship, and sharing Him together with other believers. Every moment can be a Jesus moment.

Once we finally learn the truth of that, and how incredible that life is, we deepen our daily intimacy. We seek Him more frequently during the day, and we can't get enough of prayer and studying His Word. Then, as time goes by, we find we begin to resemble Him. We do the things He would do. We care about the concerns He cares about, and most of all, we love other people on His behalf. And there's so much courage. There's nothing that can frighten us for more than a fleeting moment, because Christ has promised to go with us to the ends of the earth.

We have the courage to save that marriage. We have the courage to be better parents. We have the courage to make our careers pleasing to God. And we find ourselves speaking up for Jesus in many places. And the more we do it, the easier it is the next time. Soon it's not even courage. It's just letting Jesus live through us.

One of the great ambitions of my life is that people would say, "Look! There's a man who has been with Jesus!" I ask myself daily, *What will it take for people to be able to better see Jesus in me?*

One time, our family went to a hip, cool restaurant that employs nontraditional, highly tattooed people with multiple piercings. While Kelly stayed at the table with the kids, I went to the counter and placed our order. The young lady with colorful hair and a black T-shirt at the counter wore a necklace with an occult-looking star, and her earrings were upside-down crosses.

"Tell me about the star pendant you're wearing," I said.

"This star," she said, "is about Moses." And she proceeded to rattle off a legend about Moses that I knew was never in the Bible.

I said, "Are you a Christian?"

The question seemed distasteful to her. "No," she said. "My mom is a Christian, and I don't want to be all narrow-minded like her. I have an open mind."

"I notice you're wearing crosses as earrings—but you've got them upside down."

"I wear them like that because they get caught in my hair."

"Uh, you might want to pick a different set of earrings then."

It seemed like her appearance was asking for a spiritual conversation. But there were people in line behind me, so I had to make my next statement count.

"I just want you to know," I said, "that when I was sixteen years old, I was partying and doing wild stuff and asking questions about life, just like you are now. Some friends told me about Jesus Christ, and I placed my faith in Him to forgive my sins and take control of my life. Jesus has changed my whole life—and He loves you."

Her response? She tapped her little register, and it went *beep-boop-beep*. Then she said, "That'll be twenty-one dollars and fifty-nine cents."

Without another word to me, she began helping the next customer in line.

But I still remember her and pray for her, because the name I spoke to her has power. And my word to you is this: *be bold. Be courageous.* Day after day, with the people you meet, speak the powerful name of Jesus.

Not every encounter ends with a harvest. But you never know how or when the seed you plant may blossom.

9

Now How Much Would You Pay?

The Meaning of Sacrifice

In the winter of AD 320, Emperor Licinius ordered all Roman soldiers to offer a sacrifice to the gods. They renounced any other form of faith or they received the death penalty.

Forty brave Christian soldiers who served in Rome's elite Twelfth Legion Fulminata ("the legion armed with lightning") told their commander what their souls required. They'd gladly lay down their lives for the emperor of Rome—but forced to choose, they'd now lay down their lives for Jesus, the Emperor of heaven.

On a frozen lake, these soldiers were stripped naked. Then the commander posted guards on the shore and had these guards build a fire and prepare a warm bath. Any of the forty soldiers could save his life, walk off the ice, and enjoy the warmth of that bath; they simply had to renounce Christ.

Deep into the night, as the freezing wind whipped across the ice, the forty Christian men sang hymns and psalms together. Their voices grew weaker. Some faded to silence.

One survivor could still move. He waved to the guards on the shore. "I'll renounce Christ," he called out. "I'll sacrifice to the gods. Just let me live!" He struggled off the ice and toward the fire and the warm bath, leaving his dead or dying companions behind. But then the unthinkable happened.

A Roman guard passed him going the other way. He had seen enough. Thirty-nine men had given their lives courageously, so Jesus must be real. He threw off his clothes and took the man's place. By morning, he became the fortieth martyr.[1]

True faith in Christ is truly unstoppable. The threat of death has only tested it and shown it to be real. We understand this throughout history, including Acts 6.

An Escalation of Violence

As we've seen, the Sanhedrin told the disciples to stop talking about Jesus. The disciples ignored that command. They worshiped in plain view, preached, healed, and honored Christ. The converts continued to emerge, and the religious leaders knew they had a problem—persecute one, and several more would take his place.

Still, something had to be done. The apostles were rounded up once again and thrown in jail. It only brought about another miracle—an angel set them free during the night (see Acts 5:19–20). The angel told them to keep on keeping on—to preach the Good News at the temple.

You can imagine the high priest's rage when he was told the apostles were not in their cell and ready for trial. They were out at the temple, preaching! So again they were rounded up. And again the high priest asked them why they wouldn't obey their gag order.

The apostles replied, "We must obey God rather than men" (v. 29). They went on to explain, once again, that their present accusers had killed Jesus, that God had raised Him to His right hand, and that it was their job—by the power of the Holy Spirit—to bear witness to all of it.

The religious leaders flew into a near-murderous rage—but then a highly respected Pharisee named Gamaliel sent the apostles out of the room. He pointed out that this should be a Roman problem—let the overlords sort it all out. That's what they had done with such fanatical movements in the past. This was practical, but he also said something wise: "If this plan or this work is of men, it will be overthrown; but if it is of God, you will not be able to overthrow them. You may even be found fighting against God" (vv. 38–39). If this was just another fad, it would die on its own. But if it came from God, there was nothing the council could do to stop it.

The Sanhedrin decided to restrain themselves. Instead of executing them, they flogged the disciples and again ordered them to stop preaching about Jesus. And when the apostles were released, they went out praising God for considering them worthy of persecution. And they witnessed even more passionately.

Trial one had issued a warning. Trial two had given beatings and reissued the warning. The tension was only getting worse, from words to whips—to what?

The third trial would have to demand the ultimate price.

A Bright New Face

Acts 6 introduces us to a man named Stephen, a man of great faith and character, filled with the Holy Spirit. But wasn't everybody like that? This was the early church, right?

Wrong. It's easy to romanticize this period, and to ask why we can't be so perfect today. But the truth is that problems existed then as now. For instance, there were cultures in collision. Most early Christians were Jewish. But there were two kinds of Jews, Hebraic and Grecian or Hellenistic. The former were directly linked to the old traditions; the latter were part of the new world order, in which nations mingled and shared the common language of Greek. Outside cultures tended to seep into their faith, and not every old Hebrew tradition was prized.

In the church, widows were receiving ministerial assistance. But the Grecian widows claimed they were being neglected—that favoritism was in effect. As a result, deacons were appointed. Seven men would oversee the assistance and make sure it was fair. As it happened, one of these deacons was named Stephen.

His name tells us he was a Grecian Jew. Luke tells us more: Stephen was "full of grace and power" (Acts 6:8), and he performed signs and wonders in the name of Jesus.

What did it mean that Stephen was "full of grace"? It meant he had a deep faith and understanding of the grace Jesus offered through His death on the cross. Grace is *not* getting away with sin because someone was looking the other way. In fact, grace means you got caught red-handed, you're busted, you have no excuse, you have no way to pay the fine—yet you receive mercy and forgiveness that is completely undeserved.

God's loving grace produces gratitude and obedience. Stephen was full of grace, he preached grace, and he offered grace to others. No wonder he emerged as a leader in the early church. Yet this also meant he shared in the burden of persecution.

Stephen soon found himself in conflict with a group from the Freedmen's Synagogue. These were former slaves, descendants of Jews who had been conquered by the Romans and kept far away in captivity. They had become highly committed—even legalistic—Jews. And they didn't like what Stephen preached about grace because they were very committed to the law. A debate began, and they couldn't hold their own with Stephen's wisdom and reliance on the Holy Spirit (v. 10).

So there was a conspiracy to frame Stephen for blasphemy— a capital crime under Jewish law. They found false witnesses, then dragged him before the Sanhedrin. What had happened to Jesus was going to happen to Stephen.

The false witnesses said their lines. They accused Stephen of saying that Jesus would destroy the temple and change the law of Moses. And while the false witnesses were speaking, something amazing happened: Stephen's face shone like the face of an angel.

Oh, the irony! All those perjurers lied about Stephen, claiming he had blasphemed God and Moses—but when Stephen's face shone like the face of an angel, it undoubtedly reminded everyone of one man: Moses, whose face had shone when he came down from Mount Sinai with the tablets of the law in Exodus 34. God was sending a message.

Have you ever been around a person of truly Christlike character? That person's countenance is simply different. This person has a kind of aura because he or she *has been with Jesus*. Heavenly character produces a heavenly countenance.

Many on the Sanhedrin were undoubtedly shaken by the appearance of Stephen's radiant face. They knew their Bible, and here was one more miracle they couldn't explain away. How did they continue to resist the truth? The high priest, sensing that the mood in the room was shifting, focused everyone's attention on the task at hand—the task of framing this innocent man, shutting him up, and getting him out of the way. The high priest addressed Stephen directly and asked him if the accusations against him were true.

Which, of course, gave Stephen just the opening he wanted.

Wisdom + Power

Stephen was a preacher, all right—ask him a yes-or-no question and he preaches a sermon. The longest one in Acts, no less. It takes up almost the whole of Acts 7 and recaps virtually the entire Old Testament. Stephen was full of the Spirit—and long-winded!

We've already been told Stephen was full of grace and power, and here is the proof. The power, of course, was courtesy of the Holy Spirit, according to Acts 1:8, and it's still available to you and me. The early church did perform more signs and wonders, given by God to authenticate the Christian movement. As time went on, there were fewer dramatic miracles. But the Holy Spirit never fades. He still works through us.

One of the clearest ministries of the Spirit is to speak through us. Most committed Christians have experienced times when they suddenly had an eloquence they had never experienced, when they said just the right things at just the right times, and realized afterward the Spirit had taken the wheel. Particularly when you or I communicate the gospel, the Holy Spirit will give us the strength and the words. The more we lean on Him, the more He will draw others to Christ.

Then there's wisdom. In the past, Stephen won his arguments with the Freedmen because he depended upon the Spirit. He spoke with supernatural wisdom—and what is wisdom? It's the ability to combine knowledge, experience, common sense, and insight in order to make good decisions and give sound advice. Knowledge is a body of information, but you can have a library full and still lack wisdom. You can also be limited in facts and deep in wisdom.

The church needs men and women steeped in wisdom.

If you want to be wise, then go to God and ask Him for wisdom. This is God's promise to us: "Now if any of you lacks wisdom, he should ask God, who gives to all generously and without criticizing, and it will be given to him" (James 1:5).

Don't pray once and wait to be zapped by wisdom. Pray daily, "Lord, give me the wisdom I need for this day." Pray hourly, "Lord, give me the wisdom I need to get through this meeting, this phone call, this crisis, this confrontation." If you need wisdom in your parenting, in your marriage, in your workplace, in your church, or in your witnessing, ask God, who gives generously.

Truly, one of my most frequent prayers is for wisdom. Almost every day for the last two decades I have asked for wisdom. The stakes are too high for me, as a leader in my home, vocation, and community, to go on my own hunches. I ask for wisdom every day and God is faithful to grant it.

Wisdom is slower than the speed of thought. You may have a quick impulse to deliver a snappy comeback, to send a sharply worded email, to toss out a snarky text message. Cleverness comes quickly. Wisdom is never a knee-jerk reaction. Wisdom always wants to slow us down and mull it over—not to hit the send button too quickly but to count to ten.

Genuine wisdom also seeks wise counsel from others. Friends often see your situation more clearly than you can. Godly advisors vastly increase your chances of doing the right thing.

Depth of wisdom, however, comes from God's Word and from the Holy Spirit through prayer. Daily time spent in the Word and in prayer builds reserves of wisdom within us that will serve us well in times of crisis. Verses come to mind at the right moment as we sense God's guiding hand.

And the best part is that wisdom is available on demand. In Proverbs, Solomon pictures Wisdom as a lady who cries out to us, who begs us to listen, who tries to get our attention—but we shut our ears and ignore her:

> Wisdom calls out in the street;
> she raises her voice in the public squares. . . .
> If you respond to my warning,
> then I will pour out my spirit on you
> and teach you my words. (Prov. 1:20, 23)

Peacefully Violent

Stephen displayed grace, power, and wisdom in his response to his accusers. Yet he refused to compromise the truth. Like Peter and John, he laid the betrayal of Jesus at the feet of the Sanhedrin.

It was one time too many for the leaders to hear these words. They became a nasty mob. And Luke tells us that God did something truly remarkable. Even as the rage was boiling over and he faced death, Stephen said, "Look! I see the heavens opened and the Son of Man standing at the right hand of God!" (Acts 7:56).

Luke tells us that the members of the Sanhedrin covered their ears when Stephen said these words. They rushed him, dragged him outside the city, and stoned him.

Make no mistake, stoning is a brutal, ugly way to die. The people in the mob picked up the heaviest stones they could lift. They hurled the stones at the victim, delivering one bone-crushing blow after another until he lay dead.

Luke tells us that the witnesses of the stoning of Stephen placed their robes at the feet of a young Pharisee named Saul. It's an intriguing cameo appearance, for Saul would become the chief of persecutors, then experience his own miracle. He would be better known as the apostle Paul.

As the mob stoned Stephen, the first martyr of the church cried out in a loud voice, making two final pronouncements, both of them prayers. First, he said, "Lord Jesus, receive my spirit!" Then he spoke his last words, "Lord, do not charge them with this sin!"

"And saying this," we are told, "he fell asleep" (vv. 59–60).

He was gone, peaceful in the violence of his own death.

Lessons from Sacrifice

Sacrifice sanctifies us. It's why Jesus calls us to take up our cross and follow Him. Sacrifice is one of the routes God uses to make us more like Him. There are seven crucial similarities between the deaths of Stephen and Jesus—and each one teaches a key principle.

Principle 1: Trust the truth when others lie.

When Jesus was on trial before the high priest and the Sanhedrin, His enemies brought in false witnesses to give perjured testimony about Him. Even though the testimony was contradictory, inconsistent, and obviously false, the high priest demanded that Jesus answer the charges. Jesus kept silent.

When Stephen was on trial before the high priest and the Sanhedrin, the same thing happened. Like Jesus, Stephen did not defend himself against false accusations. Instead, he turned to the Old Testament and gave a sermon about grace.

You can't keep people from lying about you—but you don't have to play their game by their rules. Instead, trust in God's truth. Take the initiative and be God's witness for the truth.

Principle 2: Look to heaven in prayer.

When Jesus was in the garden of Gethsemane, just hours before the cross, He agonized in prayer, seeking God's will. In the same way, Stephen gazed prayerfully toward heaven and saw Jesus standing at the right hand of the Father.

Here we see a principle I've heard explained as the upper story and lower story of life. Throughout our lives, we focus on what's happening on the "first floor," here on earth. Meanwhile, another story is occurring in heaven. Spiritual forces are at work in ways we don't realize. Stephen caught a glimpse of that second story—but we can be sure it is always there. Jesus is always at the right hand of the Father. Jesus taught His disciples to pray, "Your will be done on earth as it is in heaven"—or may the first floor be in line with the second.

Nonbelievers tell us this house has only one level—but they're not leveling with us. We need to be second story–minded. How differently would the disciples have seen the crucifixion if they could have seen what heaven was doing? How differently would you see the trials in your life if you understood how God was already using them for your good?

Principle 3: The crowd usually gets it wrong.

French writer Jean Cocteau observed, "If it has to choose who is to be crucified, the crowd will always save Barabbas."[2]

It's true, isn't it? The crowd makes one bad choice after another, especially in matters of morality and spirituality.

Pontius Pilate's crowd chose Barabbas. Stephen's Sanhedrin sermon gave way to a mob bellowing like beasts and destroying an innocent man.

From time to time, step back and look at your relationship to the crowd. If you're just a face in it, fitting in with every move, then it's time to ask yourself a few questions.

Jesus said the road leading to destruction is quite wide, because quite a crowd takes it. Yet the road to eternal life is narrow and twisting. It's hard at times. It's lonely. But every step of the way, it's better than the road that Noah's generation took, than the people at the foot of Mount Sinai took as they made the golden calf, than the mobs around Jesus and Stephen took.

I tell my children to love everyone, make friends widely, but choose their Friday-night friends with care. The latter is when the really dangerous decisions are made. Beware of the crowd. Rolling with the pack usually means rolling downhill.

Principle 4: Place your eternity in God's hands.

As the mob stoned him, Stephen called out, "Lord Jesus, receive my spirit!" It's strikingly close to what Jesus said: "Father, into Your hands I entrust My spirit" (Luke 23:46).

You can safely place your eternity in the hands of the Lord Jesus Christ. Don't entrust your eternity to church membership, baptism, good works, or giving money to good causes. Those are great things, but they are no toll on the winding road to salvation.

Stephen's dying prayer is unusual because he prayed directly to Jesus. People in the Bible usually pray to God the Father—but Stephen prayed directly to Jesus: "Lord Jesus, receive my spirit!" Stephen understood that Jesus is God, and that only Jesus could open the way for him to enter heaven.

Principle 5: Forgive.

Here comes a hard one. Everyone loves forgiveness until they're called to practice it. Just imagine forgiving people while they are crucifying you or stoning you to death. Jesus and Stephen verbally forgave their own bloodstained, howling executioners.

Acts 7 ends in violence. But in the midst of this horrifying violence, Stephen dies a peaceful death. After expressing forgiveness toward his killers, he "fell asleep" (v. 60), what F. F. Bruce calls "an unexpectedly beautiful and peaceful description of so brutal a death."[3] When Luke tells us Stephen was full of grace, he means it.

Jesus, by both command and example, calls us to forgive. Have we been hurt by others? Yes, we have. Is our anger valid? Yes, it is. But Jesus calls us to follow His example and forgive. When Stephen asked the Lord to forgive the sins of his attackers, he demonstrated an amazing depth of Christlike character. We must do no less. Forgiveness brings peace, not always in the relationship but always in *us*.

Principle 6: Your trials help bring others to the truth.

Stephen's trial of being stoned to death is gruesome and frightening beyond imagination. Yet, as Stephen lay dying, a man named Saul stood by, giving his approval.

Saul watched the way Stephen died. He had probably seen Stephen's face shining during the trial before the Sanhedrin. Now he saw Stephen's courage and grace in dying.

Later, on the road to Damascus, he would have a dramatic encounter with the risen Lord Jesus. As the apostle Paul, he would understand what being a Christian was truly about, because he had been an eyewitness to the death of Stephen.

Paul was "the apostle of grace." Could it be that an earlier man of grace, Stephen, gave him his model?

Today, people are watching your life. How you go through trials will have a great impact on the people around you. If you go through suffering with a grace and a peace that passes understanding, you will impact others for Christ. You may not see it come to fruition—Stephen didn't—but trust God to grow the seeds you help plant.

Missionary Jim Elliot was twenty-eight years old when he and four fellow missionaries were murdered in January 1956 while attempting to take the gospel to the Huaorani people of Ecuador. In a journal entry dated October 28, 1949, Elliot famously wrote, "He is no fool who gives what he cannot keep to gain that which he cannot lose."[4]

Though Elliot and his companions lost their lives, their deaths impacted the Huaorani people, and many of them—including some of the very warriors who had committed the murders—came to know Christ in the wake of the tragedy. Like Stephen, his earthly life was too short but his eternal impact was immeasurable.

Principle 7: Godly sacrifice produces a heavenly celebration.

When we undergo a sacrifice on earth, heaven rejoices. Jesus was sacrificed for our sins, and heaven rings with celebration (see Rev. 7:13–17).

Just before Stephen died, the Holy Spirit gave him a glimpse into heaven. For a few moments, Stephen was able to stand in the lower story of his life, seeing into the upper story. He knew that God was using his sacrifice. Stephen saw Jesus standing at the right hand of God. What happened above was so glorious that it didn't really matter what was happening to him below.

Everything changes when we see Jesus. Notice that when Stephen looked into heaven, he didn't see Jesus *seated* at the right hand of God. He said, "Look! I see . . . the Son of Man *standing* at the right hand of God!" (Acts 7:56, emphasis added). This is an important detail. Hebrews 10:12 tells us, "But [Jesus], after offering one sacrifice for sins forever, *sat down* at the right hand of God" (emphasis added).

Why, according to Hebrews, did Jesus sit down at God's right hand? It helps to understand that the priests of the temple in Jerusalem were always standing and walking. There were no chairs in the temple. Why? Because the priest's job was never done. There was always another sacrifice to be made for the forgiveness of sin. The priest could never sit down because his job was never done.

As Jesus was dying on the cross, He said, "It is finished!" This is a profound theological statement. The priestly work of making sacrifices for sin was finally accomplished—finished once and for all. He could sit at God's right hand. So why did Stephen see Jesus standing?

First, Jesus was probably welcoming Stephen into heaven as the first Christian martyr. He was saying to Stephen, "Welcome home. I've got you. You're safe here."

Second, Jesus may have been acknowledging Stephen before God. Jesus once said, "Therefore, everyone who will acknowledge Me before men, I will also acknowledge him before My Father in heaven" (Matt. 10:32).

148

Stephen was being handled brutally by men, yet he was honored before God—honored by Jesus Himself. The upper story completely changes how we understand the lower. We understand our eternal impact—and the upper story changes *our* story.

Paying Full Price

I'm Texas born and bred, so I know the meaning of "Remember the Alamo!"

I have toured the Alamo Mission in San Antonio. The exhibits present such a glorious history of the great siege that it's easy to forget that the Texan defenders *lost* that battle. During the thirteen days of the attack in 1836, troops under General Antonio López de Santa Anna killed every desperate Texan—approximately two hundred men.

Why do we remember a battle that was lost? We remember because the defeat at the Alamo gave birth to the victory at San Jacinto.

A little more than a month and a half after all the defenders of the Alamo were slaughtered, forces led by General Sam Houston (my city's namesake) met Santa Anna's army at San Jacinto on April 21, 1836—a decisive victory of the Texas Revolution. The battle lasted all of eighteen minutes, resulting in the death of 630 of Santa Anna's soldiers and the capture of 730 more. Only nine Texans were killed. The Republic of Texas became an independent nation, and in 1845 was annexed as the twenty-eighth state of the USA. (Interestingly, our church formed in 1841, meaning that we were a church four years before Texas was a state.)

The death of Stephen is much like the defeat at the Alamo. Stephen's death triggered a wave of persecution against the early church. The early Christians were stoned, crucified, thrown to wild animals, and subjected to many other horrors. The result? The church grew even more rapidly. The early Christians did not lay down their lives in vain. God used them powerfully.

Strangely enough, the church strengthens and grows in persecution yet gets into trouble in times of prosperity. Persecution spreads Christians outward into the world, fulfilling Mission 1:8. Prosperity makes the church smug and complacent. It causes the church to lose its dependence on God and its passion for those in need.

Opposition causes Christians to depend on only God. It drives us into the arms of the Lord. That's why, as the apostle Paul says, "For when I am weak, then I am strong" (2 Cor. 12:10)—and why second-century church father Tertullian wrote, "The blood of the martyrs is the seed of the Church."[5]

Do you think persecution is a dusty page out of Christian history? It has happened more frequently during the past one hundred years than in all other centuries combined. Persecution is a way of life for Christians in many parts of the world. We easily forget there is a price to be paid for following Christ—and as we move deeper into this post-Christian era, we may yet have to pay that price here on American soil.

We don't invite misery and suffering. We have no weird death wish. But we understand that Jesus never promised a life of ease and prosperity to His followers. He promised that we would have tribulation, and we know we can't lose anyway—to live is Christ, and to die is gain (see Phil. 1:21).

You may never be asked to physically give your life for Christ. But living as a believer raises the likelihood of social and vocational persecution. We are called to live each day sacrificially—whatever sacrifice may be required to glorify God. When I hear stories of martyrs, I realize the depth and relevance and eternal nature of Christianity. I may not enjoy the struggles that may arise, but if God's kingdom increases in some way, I realize that's what counts. I try to keep my faith fixed on the upper story—to set my mind on eternal things. That's where the battle is being won, in the realm of "the spiritual forces of evil in the heavens" (Eph. 6:12). That's where celebration breaks out when we make a sacrifice for the unstoppable gospel.

I think about that story of the forty men who froze to death on the ice. One moment there was a deathly chill, and the next a warm embrace. They were in the arms of the Father—and there they'll remain throughout eternity. Perhaps they looked up to see Jesus standing, welcoming them with the words, "Well done, good and faithful servant."

What sacrifice will you endure today, in your longing to hear those words?

10

New and Lasting

When God Transforms

Bryan and Wanda are proof of the power of the gospel to change lives. Some years ago, they met at a Houston care center for homeless people. Both were going through hard times. Wanda had recently left an abusive marriage and now was working at the care center. Bryan had just arrived from Louisiana and had nowhere else to go.

Bryan and Wanda began dating. Soon after that, a friend of Wanda's encouraged her to visit the downtown campus of Houston's First Baptist Church. The love she felt from our church family captured her heart. She told Bryan about our church and they began attending together. Soon they became engaged, and the entire church family at the downtown campus surrounded them with love.

Wanda and Bryan on
their wedding day.

The members of our church donated everything Bryan and Wanda needed for their wedding, including premarital counseling; wedding coordinators; Wanda's wedding dress, hair styling, and makeup; wedding rings; decorations and flowers for the ceremony; a wedding cake; a wedding photographer; and a four-day honeymoon at a beachfront resort in Galveston. Our campus pastor even chauffeured them to the resort and back since they had no car.

The bride walked down the aisle on the arm of their Bible study teacher, and when asked, "Who gives this woman in marriage?" he replied, "Her church family and I."

The wedding was covered by *The Houston Chronicle*, ABC's *Good Morning America*, the *Huffington Post*, and other news media. As Wanda told ABC News, "The church is so loving and so kind. I was speechless. I found myself in tears a lot of times because I just didn't think anyone could love me that much." [1]

Today, Wanda is a social worker and Bryan is in the construction and remodeling trade. Both are deeply involved in the ministry of our church and in awe of how God has transformed their lives. That's what the unstoppable gospel is all about—transformed lives. Only within the church do you hear such stories! As the apostle Paul wrote, "Therefore, if anyone is in Christ, he is a new creation; old things have passed away, and look, new things have come" (2 Cor. 5:17).

People *can* change. By the power of God, human beings can do a complete 180. As Exhibit A, I submit the story of the apostle Paul himself.

From Terrorist to Evangelist

To understand the radical change that occurred in Paul, you have to understand who he had been. To understand the grace of God in his life, you have to grasp the rage that had been in his heart.

Stephen's body was scarcely in the ground when Saul launched a campaign of terror against the church. Saul of Tarsus was an angry, self-righteous Pharisee. Like the terrorists of today, he could commit brutal violence against people simply because their beliefs differed from his—and he'd have no pangs of conscience afterward. Saul watched Stephen's body being smashed and shattered, his bones broken—and Luke underlines the fact that he *gave approval* to this brutality, believing that this gruesome execution pleased God.

Saul wanted to destroy the church and wipe Christianity off the face of the earth. Luke said that Saul "was ravaging the church" (Acts 8:3). The Greek word for "ravaging," *lymainō*, conveys a strong sense of destruction, devastation, and ruin, like a wild boar despoiling a vineyard.

But God was about to transform Saul of Tarsus. This violent man was about to become God's apostle of grace, His ambassador of peace. When Paul wrote his letter to the Galatians, he told the story of his former life. "I persecuted God's church to an extreme degree and tried to destroy it," he said. "But when

God . . . called me by His grace, [He] was pleased to reveal His Son in me" (Gal. 1:13, 15–16).

It could not have been easy for the apostle Paul to live with his pre-conversion memories. The images of Stephen's death probably came back to haunt him, filling him with shame and guilt. Perhaps, in his nightmares, he saw the faces of all the men and women and children he'd had dragged away to prison.

Maybe there are pre-Christian events from your life that still trouble you late at night. We know God has forgiven us, but can we forgive ourselves? Though Paul was an apostle of grace, he must have struggled with self-forgiveness. He probably had to remind himself many times: "Therefore, no condemnation now exists for those in Christ Jesus" (Rom. 8:1).

If you question whether God has forgiven you, or if you struggle to forgive yourself, then the apostle Paul is your patron saint, your role model. God forgave Saul and transformed him into the apostle Paul. God wants to transform your life as well.

We often feel God is, at best, mildly disappointed with us when, in fact, He has completely forgiven us. If there is no condemnation in Christ—there is no condemnation at all. Stop beating yourself up when there are so many positive things you could be doing with that emotional energy. Let the grace of Jesus Christ transform your thinking.

This certainly happened to Paul. He endorsed the death of Stephen, then imitated him. He hated Stephen's preaching of Christ in the synagogues, then he devoted his life to doing it himself. He stood with the Pharisees who rejected Stephen's message, then he stood against the Pharisees and repeated it. And some time after Stephen was stoned to death, Paul was stoned and left for dead (see Acts 14:19; 2 Cor. 11:25). Church tradition says he died as a martyr, just as Stephen had done.

In their wildest dreams, no one present at the killing of Stephen could have imagined that Saul of Tarsus, the man holding the garments, would take Stephen's place as the dynamic spokesman for Christianity. It was simply unthinkable.

Which glorified God all the more. Grace transformed Saul of Tarsus into the apostle Paul. The grace of God can turn a terrorist into an evangelist and a ravager of the church into its champion and chief visionary.

A Tale of Transformation

Adoniram Judson was born in 1788, the son of a Congregationalist minister in Massachusetts. A brilliant student, Judson attended the College of Rhode Island (now Brown University) at age sixteen. He graduated as class valedictorian at age nineteen. While at college, Judson befriended a young skeptic named Jacob Eames. The influence of Eames pushed Judson away from the faith he had learned as a boy.

Once, during a journey, Judson stopped at an inn for the night. There was only one room available. As Judson tried to sleep, he was disturbed by the cries of a violently ill man in the next room. The next morning, Judson learned that the man had died—and that his name was Jacob Eames.

Judson was sure it was no coincidence that he had heard the death throes of the man who had led him away from his faith. Judson believed God had appointed him to be in that room for a reason—and the reason was to call him back to Christ. In life, Eames had led him to doubt; in death, to faith.

Judson dedicated himself to following wherever Christ would lead. He enrolled at Andover Theological Seminary and prepared for a career as a missionary. He and his wife, Ann, arrived in Rangoon, Burma, in 1813, and began working among the Burmese people.

During his first seven years in Burma, Adoniram Judson saw one conversion. By 1823, after a full decade of labor among the Burmese people, only eighteen had come to Christ. In 1824, England and Burma went to war, and Judson was arrested on suspicion of being a British spy. He was marched barefoot over rough terrain for miles, then imprisoned in one of the worst prisons in the world.

He was shackled, tortured, starved, and often trussed up and suspended upside-down for days. Ann worked tirelessly to win his release—then, just weeks after he was finally freed, she died of illness and stress.

After Ann's death, Judson entered a depression that lasted more than a year. Considering himself a failure, he even dug a grave beside his jungle hut and pictured himself lying in it. But after that year of mourning and depression, Judson began to regain his passion for evangelism.

In 1828, Judson was working among a Burmese tribe called the Karen people when he met Ko Tha Byu, a robber who admitted killing at least thirty men. He was the worst of the worst, yet Judson and others led him to the Lord and baptized him—and the former robber immediately became like the apostle Paul, preaching the gospel to his own people.

It's fascinating to learn that these tribal people had a number of traditions that echoed the Old Testament. The Karen people believed in one eternal, all-powerful God who created the heavens and the earth, who created the first man and formed the first woman from a rib taken from the man. They believed that humanity had been tempted into sin by a devil, and they awaited the coming of a messiah. Their traditions even spoke of white-skinned strangers who would come to them, bringing a sacred "parchment roll" of Scripture. They were primed to receive the gospel.

Judson's one convert among the Karen people, the reformed robber Ko Tha Byu, was a tireless evangelist. By 1831, he had established a Karen church with more than one hundred members. By the time Ko Tha Byu died in 1840, there were more than 1,200 Karen Christians. By 1856, the number of baptized Karen Christians had reached almost 12,000.[2] The Karen Christian population is still influential in Burma (now Myanmar) today.

Adoniram Judson and his second wife, Sarah, had a son named Edward, and he became a pastor in New York City, leading a church once known as Memorial Baptist, now Judson Memorial, in lower Manhattan. During Edward's first seven years as pastor, seven hundred people were added to the congregation—a sharp contrast to the single Burmese convert his father made in the same span of time.

Edward Judson once spoke about the sense of tragedy and failure that overshadowed much of his father's missionary career. He offered this insight: "If we succeed without suffering it is because others suffered before us; if we suffer without succeeding, it is that others may succeed after us."[3]

Adoniram Judson was far from a failure. He left behind churches, new believers, and evangelists, including his son Edward and a Karen tribesman who became a Burmese apostle Paul. Judson left a legacy that provides inspiration today. The church needs more unstoppable pioneers like Adoniram Judson who are willing to pay the price and leave a legacy of transformed lives for others to follow. We can't see in the present what God has planned for the future. Generations will reap what you and I sow. What will our legacy to the future be?

Should I Stay or Should I Go?

Stephen couldn't have imagined his own legacy. But on the day of his stoning, it seemed to be one of persecution. Suddenly, if you were a Christian, Jerusalem wasn't a safe place for your family to live. Though the apostles stayed, many other believers scattered out into Judea and Samaria. The winds of persecution spread the seeds of faith far and wide.

We need a new idea of missionaries. We tend to think in terms of the stereotype: someone who travels across the ocean to work in some danger zone, spreading the gospel. And we feel so ordinary compared to those heroes. God doesn't see it like that. Today, as in Jerusalem, there are some who stay and some who go—but all are on a mission. All are ambassadors of Christ, both foreign and domestic.

To God, there's no difference between you and me and a full-time missionary, except that a missionary sometimes has an overseas address. Every Christian is on a mission from God to be His witness. Every Christian is, by definition, a missionary. Wherever any Christian goes is, by definition, a mission field. The earth is a mission field, and that's the meaning of Mission 1:8.

In Acts 8, the unstoppable gospel earthquake is rolling out from Jerusalem to Judea and Samaria—and the Good News is being carried by ordinary believers like you and me. Christians in the first century did not see the church divided into "clergy" and "laypeople." Everyone in the church had a transformation story to tell. Whether in the first century or the twenty-first century, all believers are called to be witnesses and to have an active part in the Lord's mission.

There are basically four choices in regards to missions:

- Giving
- Going
- Praying
- Disobeying

Missions and outreach aren't about location or personality, they are about the heart. Our hearts should land on giving, going, and praying—but run from disobeying. If you can't go you can give, and if you can't give you can pray. The joy comes when all three are in play consistently. Think about the interplay of these choices in your life. Give, go, and pray, and you'll be following Paul's path—here, there, or anywhere.

It was merely a matter of "here" for the first group of Christians. Jerusalem was where it was at, period, and the believers told their friends and neighbors about Jesus. But once the persecution began, they began to flee into the Judean hillsides and Samaria to escape persecution—and the message had legs.

We can't forget: even when the worst crises come, God is always doing something. The stoning of Stephen was a great tragedy for the church until it was clearly a great tool in the hands of God. Saul's ravaging of the church seemed devastating until it led to his soul being ravaged by God.

Acts 8:4 tells us, "So those who were scattered went on their way preaching the message of good news." The word *scattered* in the original Greek text does not suggest dust scattered to the wind but rather seed scattered on soil where it can take root and produce a harvest.

How easily we forget that the worst men can offer is nothing against the strength of God. Everything plotted in Satan's book is turned upside-down and inside-out, and becomes part of God's plan.

From High Horse to Humble Servant

Acts 9 is a turning point in the history of the unstoppable gospel. We've met Saul of Tarsus, the chief persecutor of the church. If you told the first-century Christians that Saul would become a great Christian evangelist and would write at least thirteen of the twenty-seven books of the New Testament, they'd never believe you. Imagine if the leader of Al Qaeda became the next Billy Graham.

Johnny Hunt, pastor of First Baptist Church in Woodstock, Georgia, described the paradox of the apostle Paul: "Christianity has never had a more dangerous enemy than Saul of Tarsus, or a more dedicated friend than Paul the Apostle; both are the same man."[4]

Warren Wiersbe, former pastor of Chicago's Moody Church, once wrote, "The conversion of Saul of Tarsus, the leading persecutor of the Christians, was perhaps the greatest event in church history after the coming of the Spirit at Pentecost."[5]

As Acts 9 opens, Luke tells us "Saul was still breathing threats and murder against the disciples of the Lord" (v. 1). The Greek verb Luke used here for "breathing" is *empneō*, which means "inhale," not "exhale." Luke deliberately chose that word to create a word picture of Saul inhaling threats, intoxicated by his own rage. He believed his hatred of Christians was a righteous service to God.

In John 16:2, Jesus says, "A time is coming when anyone who kills you will think he is offering service to God." The Lord's words were true in Saul's day and they are still true today. Even now, there are thousands of terrorists, motivated by religious fanaticism, who believe that slaughtering "infidels" is an act of worship to God. They are intoxicated by their own rage and deceived in their doctrine. That was the mindset of Saul of Tarsus.

Saul went to the high priest—the same high priest who had condemned Jesus—and received letters authorizing him to round up Christians and bring them back to Jerusalem as prisoners. While Saul was on the road to Damascus, a bright light flashed around him. Luke doesn't tell us the time of day in Acts 9, but in Acts 22:6, as Paul gives his testimony, he tells us that this bright light occurred at noontime. This light was *brighter* than the noonday sun! Stunned, Saul fell to the ground.

Luke doesn't tell us whether Saul was on horseback or on foot. We don't know if, when Saul fell to the ground, he fell off a horse. Yet that is traditionally the way the scene is depicted. Many artists have painted the Damascus road incident— Michelangelo, Rubens, Caravaggio, Rafael, and many more— and they all show Paul falling from a horse. Whether or not this is *historically* accurate, it's at least *symbolically* accurate. At the moment the light flashed and Saul fell to the ground, he was (figuratively and perhaps literally) knocked off his high horse. He was humbled. His self-righteous arrogance was shattered.

What happened to Saul could happen to any of us. God can take us from a high horse to a humble servant really quickly. One moment we're riding high—and the next instant we're flat on our backs in the middle of the road. That's not the kind of transformation we are looking for. We must choose to either humble ourselves before the Lord or be humbled *by* the Lord. I'd rather humble myself proactively than wait to be knocked down, wouldn't you?

As Paul lay on the ground, he heard a voice say, "Saul, Saul, why are you persecuting Me?" (Acts 9:4).

When God repeats someone's name, he's trying to get that person's attention. That's why God called from the burning bush, "Moses! Moses!" (Exod. 3:4). That's why God called to the future prophet of Israel, "Samuel! Samuel!" (1 Sam. 3:10).

Here in Acts, Jesus says, "Saul, Saul, why are you persecuting Me?" The Lord had to penetrate Saul's prideful armor to reach his heart.

"Who are You, Lord?" Saul asked.

"I am Jesus, the One you are persecuting," the Lord replied. "But get up and go into the city, and you will be told what you must do" (Acts 9:5–6).

Saul got up and opened his eyes—but he was blind. His servants took him by the hand and led him into the city of Damascus, much as a parent leads a little child. This is another symbol of Saul's humbled state. No longer on a tirade, he was now led like a toddler. In order for Saul of Tarsus to become the apostle Paul, all of his self-righteous, pharisaic pride had to be drained out of him. The humble spirit of Paul's letters proves that it worked.

Writing to the Corinthians, Paul said, "For I am the least of the apostles, unworthy to be called an apostle, because I persecuted the church of God" (1 Cor. 15:9). And, "I persecuted God's church to an extreme degree and tried to destroy it" (Gal. 1:13). These are not words of false humility. Paul was deeply ashamed of having persecuted the church—and having persecuted his Lord.

When Jesus said, "I am Jesus, the One you are persecuting," He was telling Saul that he was not merely persecuting the church, he was persecuting Jesus Himself. You might have heard an angry dad say, "If you mess with my kids, you're messing with me." Anyone who persecutes the church must answer to God for that. The Lord is our defender, and He feels every one of our wounds. These words are a great comfort to the church, but it can also be frightening to consider their implications. *When we sin—any kind of sin—we sin against God.* We might sin against our boss by padding the expense account. Or against our spouse by a telling a lie. Or against the government by "fudging" on our tax returns. But no matter who we sin against on a human level, we always sin against God.

God went to great lengths to get Saul's attention—a blinding light, calling his name twice, knocking him flat on his back, and finally, leaving him unable to eat or drink for three days. Saul had a rough few days, but understand that he had a lot of rough edges that needed sanding, a lot of pride to break down, a lot of incorrect beliefs to weed out. We think of Paul's transformation as happening in the wink of an eye with a blinding light on the road, but imagine the pain he dealt with during those three days.

In short, God needed to get his attention, and now He had it. Saul was finally ready to sit quietly and listen to what the Lord had to say.

My wife, Kelly, and I once took our kids to Walt Disney World in Florida. While there, I saw a skywriting airplane over the park. In trails of white smoke against a clear blue sky, the airplane formed the words INVITE JESUS. I burst out laughing.

Kelly looked at me like I was crazy. "What's funny about 'Invite Jesus'?"

"It just hit me," I said, "that somebody probably got up this morning and said, 'Unless I see it written in the sky, I refuse to believe in Jesus.'"

Be careful what you ask for!

And whom you persecute. There are people all around us just like Saul—proud, angry, and hateful toward Jesus and his church. Like Saul, they would like nothing better than to silence every Christian, shut down every church, tear down every cross, and stop the unstoppable gospel in its tracks. And when we hear about them, we'd like to counterattack—but, thankfully, God isn't as intimidated as us. He is after the aggressor's heart, and that aggressor may be playing right into His hands.

People like Bryan and Wanda are all around us too—people in need of love and ministry, just waiting for someone to reach out to help. "Truly, there are more people interested in spiritual conversations than Christians who want to have them."[6] Our job is to give, go, and pray, trusting God is at work, up to something great.

And don't forget God is transforming you all the while. He is working in you as He is working through you. God has a way of multitasking life change in both the giver and receiver.

The early church embraced God's transformation of ordinary human clay into monuments of His grace, a living testimony of His power. When we yield to the same, the list of great saints in heaven might just read: Stephen, Adoniram and Edward Judson, Paul—and you!

11

Connecting the Dots

Following the Divine Line

If you have children, you're familiar with "dot-to-dot" or "connect-the-dots" puzzles. The dots on the puzzle are numbered, and if you draw lines connecting the dots in the proper sequence an image will be revealed.

Children's menus at restaurants frequently have dot-to-dot puzzles to help kids pass the time until their meal arrives. These usually aren't much of a challenge with only thirty or so dots to connect, so we bought our son a book called *Extreme Dot-to-Dot*—you know, for the hardcore dot-to-dot adventurer.

One puzzle has more than 1,100 dots to connect. When you're finished, you have a map of the world. Another page has 889 dots, depicting Neil Armstrong standing on the moon in his space suit and helmet.

How many dots would it take to reveal the picture of your life's meaning? God does have a way of arranging events, one connecting to the next. And no one would dispute that life can be a puzzle.

We all have days when the dots don't connect and everything seems like a hopeless jumble. Later, however, you have perspective. You can step back and *voilà*! So *that's* what this was all about!

As Paul writes in his letter to the Romans:

> Oh, the depth of the riches
> both of the wisdom and the knowledge of God!
> How unsearchable His judgments
> and untraceable His ways! (Rom. 11:33)

God's ways are untraceable—but sometimes you can look back and catch just a glimpse of what He was up to. You can see the people and events that God connects so that your life takes on a beautiful, meaningful pattern.

In Acts 9 and 10, we see how God connects the dots in the lives of two great apostles, Paul and Peter—and in our lives as well.

Frightfully Obedient

In Acts 9:10, we meet a friend of God named Ananias. He lives in Damascus, so he has probably fled Jerusalem during the persecution. The Lord calls to him in a vision: "Ananias!" Notice He only has to say his name once, rather than twice as it was for Saul.

Ananias replies, "Here I am, Lord," which is the best answer when God speaks. It's the response of humility and readiness to serve.

"Get up and go to the street called Straight," the Lord said to him, "to the house of Judas, and ask for a man from Tarsus named Saul, since he is praying there. In a vision he has seen a man named Ananias coming in and placing his hands on him so he can regain his sight." (Acts 9:11–12)

Ananias is a little uncertain. *Saul of Tarsus? Really?* He tells God what he has heard about the fury of Saul the persecutor, particularly that Saul is on his way here with permission from the chief priests to gather up all the believers. And the Lord reaffirms His command, telling Ananias that He has chosen Saul as His messenger to the non-Jewish world, and that He will show Saul "how much he must suffer for My name!" (v. 16).

We can be certain God called his most courageous servant for a task like this one. Ananias had to take God at His Word and ignore all the gossip. His doubts about Saul took a backseat to his faith in God. Ananias would be an important "dot" in the picture of Saul that God was creating. Let's notice three steps of faith that Ananias took:

Step one: *Ananias was willing.* He prayed, "Here I am, Lord." He had a trusting faith, and he was ready to pray, give, or go wherever God sent him.

Step two: *Ananias admitted his fear.* He was honest in prayer. God answered Ananias and fortified his courage by revealing more of what He intended.

Step three: *Ananias was obedient.* He didn't sleep on it; he didn't hesitate. He left his house, went to the street called Straight, and did his job.

Do you find yourself in the place of Ananias right now? Are you *willing* to answer God's call—but *afraid*? Then do what Ananias did—admit your fear. Confess it to God and ask Him for the courage to obey. Then put one foot in front of the other and do what God has called you to do.

Ananias found Saul and addressed him as a brother in the Lord. "Brother Saul," he said, "the Lord Jesus, who appeared to you on the road you were traveling, has sent me so that you can regain your sight and be filled with the Holy Spirit" (v. 17).

At that moment, Luke writes, something like fish scales peeled away from Paul's eyes and he regained his sight. Then he arose and was baptized—*then* had lunch. For this new convert, following Jesus was more important than his physical sustenance. He was dining on something different now.

Under New Management

When Ananias came, he didn't have to lead Saul to Christ. Saul was already a believer. That's why Ananias said to him, "*Brother* Saul, regain your sight." Ananias knew that Saul, the former persecutor, had become his dear brother in Christ. So after Saul was healed, Ananias said, "Why delay? Get up and be baptized" (Acts 22:16).

Saul and Paul were the same man, at least physically. Paul had the same fingerprints, the same DNA, and the same picture on his driver's license as Saul. Yet they were also very different people. God is in the business of radically changing people—and no one has ever experienced a more radical transformation than this man.

As a new Christian, Saul was eager to share the Good News of Jesus Christ. He immediately went to the synagogues in Damascus and began preaching. Imagine the audience's confusion—*Isn't this the pest controller sent from Jerusalem, and now he's speaking in favor of the pests?* He went from the top Jesus hater to the top Jesus promoter, seemingly overnight.

When Jesus comes into our lives, He doesn't want us to add Him on like a spare room. He wants to be the foundation of a whole new house. Has Jesus become your new foundation? Has He radically transformed the way you look at the world?

Do you look at your life through the distorting lens of this dying world—or from Christ's perspective? Are you living your life with the goals of acquiring status in the community, financial security, promotions and advancement in your company, and a secure retirement? Or are you living to reach your family, friends, and neighbors with the gospel of Jesus Christ? If you've committed yourself to Jesus, the world should notice a shocking difference.

It is odd to be a pastor in my hometown. I know two distinct groups of people: those who know me as Pastor Gregg and are shocked that I sin—and those who know the pre-Christian, high school Gregg and are shocked that I am a pastor.

I once went to Houston's William P. Hobby Airport to pick up my ticket for a flight. When I got to the counter, I recognized the lady behind it as a former high school classmate. She recognized me too, and said, "I haven't seen you since graduation! Where are you flying?"

"I'm going to speak at a Christian camp for young people."

She gave me one of those bewildered looks. *This guy—speaking at a Christian camp? Maybe he's pulling my leg.*

"Wow!" she said. "I wouldn't have thought—"

"I know!" I said. "Back in school, I wouldn't have thought it either. But now Jesus lives inside me and He's changed my life."

"That's really cool," she said, handing me my ticket.

As I walked away, I prayed, "Thank You, Lord, that You changed me. And thank You for opportunities to talk about You."

Paul's Winning Streak

Paul sent shockwaves through Damascus. He preached about Jesus the Messiah as the rabbis and other religious leaders furiously debated him. Luke shows us, with each confrontation, Paul "grew more capable" (9:22) and began dominating the debates. The leaders couldn't fight the fact that the ancient Scriptures backed up everything Paul said.

Once again, as before, there was an opportunity for leaders to rethink their old assumptions. Instead, they simply decided Paul needed to die. He had to get out of town quickly. His friends lowered him in a large basket through an opening in the city wall.

Paul went to Jerusalem, where he discovered that the Christians were still afraid of him. But Barnabas, whose name means "son of encouragement," stepped forward as his advocate. Barnabas was another "dot" that God placed in the pattern of Paul's life—and such an important one. Imagine the well-known persecutor of Christians coming back to Jerusalem. He needed someone to have his back in that city. If the divine line hadn't connected this dot, would Paul have gone on to the future we know he had? Barnabas couldn't possibly have understood the impact on the future he was having, simply by being the quiet type who says, "I'm with you—let's get this done." We could use a few more like him in all our churches.

There was a far more prominent dot, however: Peter. Paul spent fifteen days with him (see Gal. 1:18). Paul did his thing, preaching in the Jerusalem synagogues and debating the religious leaders. And predictably enough, fresh conspiracies against him resulted. Paul had to be hustled out of Jerusalem and back to Tarsus. And he must have said, "So this is how my brothers and sisters in Christ felt when I persecuted them."

And there was peace, at least for a time. The gospel was unstoppable, and the church continued to grow and spread (see Acts 9:31). God's picture was coming into line—dot to dot, city to city, the gospel to the whole world.

Paul's new friends were old enemies, and his new enemies were his old friends. But Paul's oldest "friend" of all, the Word of God, was speaking to him and for him in a way it never had in the past. Acts 9:22 says that Paul was "proving" that Jesus is the Messiah—not claiming, not supposing. His opponents had no answers for his application of the ancient prophecies.

They said, "If you can't beat 'em, join 'em." Or, we might add, "beat 'em *bodily*." That's what kept happening as Paul won the arguments. He took beatings, he took verbal abuse, he had to fear for his life. As William Barclay put it, "No one persecutes a man who is ineffective."[1]

Ben Stuart succeeded me as director of Breakaway Ministries in College Station, Texas. He wrote an important book about James's epistle called *This Changes Everything*. He observes,

> When I first read the works of the modern atheists, I anticipated encountering an intimidating display of cold, hard logic. What I discovered was quite the opposite. The modern atheist does not reason; he yells. He does not seek to refute Christianity but to berate and destroy it.[2]

This was true also with the persecution Paul was receiving—no finely nuanced rebuttal, but vengeance.

From Paul to Peter: Something New

God was connecting other dots at the same time. We see it in Acts 10 with Peter and Cornelius. Cornelius, Luke tells us, was a centurion of the Italian Regiment, but a God-fearing one who led his household in devotion as well as in kindness toward the Jews (Acts 10:2). A Roman centurion adopting Judaism was highly unusual, but it happened. Cornelius believed in God and served God's people, but he didn't know God in his heart. The "head and hands" way goes over quite well socially, yet no one sees what's inside us. We can have the head knowledge and a great record of service, but the soul is the final frontier. God alone looks upon it, and He wanted Cornelius's heart.

An angel comes to Cornelius in a vision, commends him for his service, and sends him on an errand to Peter, who is lodging with a man named Simon. Cornelius sends two servants and one soldier. And even as that delegation travels, Peter has a vision of his own. It's about noon, and Peter is on the roof praying as his hosts prepare lunch downstairs. Peter sees heaven opening and a great sheet descending with mammals, reptiles, and birds. A voice says, "Get up, Peter; kill and eat!" (v. 13).

Peter protests. He is a good Jew who has kept the dietary laws, which this act would violate. The voice replies, "What God has made clean, you must not call common" (v. 15). It happens again, and then a third time before the sheet and its contents disappear into heaven.

It's interesting how often Peter says no to the Lord in the Gospels—and here. When Jesus says he will be taken and killed, Peter says no (see Mark 8:31–33). When Jesus begins to wash the feet of the disciples, Peter protests (see John 13:6–8). And when Jesus predicts His disciples will turn away from Him, again Peter contradicts Him (see Matt. 26:31–35). In Acts, Peter does it yet again: "No, Lord!"

No + Lord: that's actually an oxymoron, a contradiction in terms. "Lord" presupposes a *yes* answer, doesn't it? You can't say no to your Master.

Yet here, even after the Spirit has taken hold of his life, Peter thinks in terms of old paradigms. The meaning of the vision was that God was doing a new thing. It wasn't about food—it was about *people*.

Peter also had a pattern of needing three lessons to learn something. He denied Jesus three times, and Jesus reinstated him with three affirmations in John 21, "Feed my lambs . . . shepherd my sheep . . . Feed my sheep" (vv. 15–19). Now he needs a three-peat of his vision.

All his life, Peter was taught that God's program in history was for the Jews. He'd been given Mission 1:8, but he still saw a *Jewish* gospel, to be preached to Jewish people, not to "unclean" Gentiles. The gospel is moving dot-to-dot from the Jews to the Samaritans to the Gentiles, but Peter is still drawing the old lines. God is always doing something new.

New Men, New Realities

Peter is struggling with this vision as the Spirit tells him about the three men soon to arrive. Peter is to accept them and go with them with no more, "No, Lord." Just do it. So when Peter hears about Cornelius, and receives an invitation from him to come and speak, he falls in line with God's will. And as he arrives at their destination, Cornelius falls at his feet as if Peter were a god.

Peter tells him to stand up—he's just a man (see Acts 10:26). So the host explains his own vision to Peter and lets him know that he has gathered his whole home to hear what the apostle has to say.

Peter makes a declaration: "Now I really understand that God doesn't show favoritism, but in every nation the person who fears Him and does righteousness is acceptable to Him" (vv. 34–35). And Peter goes on to share the greatest story ever told, the best news ever shared—and the Holy Spirit, we're told, comes upon the household.

Here are Peter and Cornelius, a Jew and a Roman, who have had their minds turned around and rearranged by God. For both of them, the reality of the gospel, and its movement from Jew to Gentile, is a shocking one.

Cornelius is a good man who sees religion as so many acts of kindness. He now must realize that all those good works are worthless for salvation. No matter how good they are, our works amount to so many filthy rags before the perfection of the Lord. Only Jesus could do the "good work" of salvation.

Peter already knew about Jesus. His new reality was that Jesus was for everyone—even a non-Jew who happened to be a Roman. It defied everything taught to him and his ancestors.

One for All

Peter's message to Cornelius and his family is recorded in Acts 10:34–43. Peter reviews the coming of Jesus and how the message of salvation came through the Jews, how Jesus was crucified and raised on the third day, how the disciples saw Him and shared meals with Him, and finally, how Jesus commissioned the disciples to spread the Good News. "Through His name everyone who believes in Him will receive forgiveness of sins," he concludes (v. 43).

Let's break it down.

1. The gospel is the Good News of peace.

Peter affirms this is *not* the good news of health, wealth, personal success, social justice, or political change. The Good News of Jesus is this: peace between God and humanity. What could be better?

There's a lot of confusion about this—people shopping for the wrong item. Stephen wouldn't agree that the gospel brings health and wealth. Peter, as he was later crucified upside down, would argue with the gospel being about justice. Paul, sitting in his prison, would have affirmed that nearly everything can be taken away from us but *peace with God*. That's Good News—that brings more good news. Once we're at peace with Him, we find the way to experience peace with each other. God connects the dots.

Peace with God is also good for the soul, for mental and emotional health. The gospel is not about motivation, but it ultimately motivates us. It's not about "success," but those who are at peace with God find that their self-made problems melt away and success is more possible.

Peace with God makes us more caring, more concerned with justice. It makes all things possible. But the true Good News is that our sins are forgiven; our souls need no longer be in turmoil because we've declared a truce in our war with heaven.

Psalm 119:165 tells us, "Abundant peace belongs to those who love Your instruction; nothing makes them stumble." Proverbs 16:7 says, "When a man's ways please the LORD, He makes even his enemies to be at peace with him." Paul, in Colossians 1:19–20, wrote, "For God was pleased to have all His fullness dwell in [Jesus], and through Him to reconcile everything to Himself by making peace through the blood of His cross—whether things on earth or things in heaven." And in Ephesians 2:14, Paul wrote, "For He is our peace, who made both groups one and tore down the dividing wall of hostility."

Peace with God makes victory possible in every war we fight: with others, with ourselves, even with other nations. Someday, when the Prince of Peace reigns, the dream of world peace will become a reality.

Peace comes when we acknowledge that Jesus is Lord. As Peter tells Cornelius, God has sent the Good News of peace through Jesus Christ—He is Lord of all. That means no more of the "No, Lord" mentality. The peace of God means life becomes one great, affirming *yes.*

2. The gospel is the Good News that the resurrection of Jesus changes everything.

It changes our *present*. Because Jesus rose from the grave, we are justified before God, we have new life, we are adopted into God's family, and we have meaning and purpose for living.

It changes our *future*. Because Jesus rose from the grave, the power of death has been destroyed. This is a key truth I share when I officiate a funeral. Without hope that the person has been raised to eternal life we are hopeless. D. L. Moody said, "One day you will read in the papers D. L. Moody of East Northfield, is dead. Don't you believe a word of it! At that time I shall be more alive than I am now."[3]

The resurrection even changes our *past*. Because Jesus rose from the grave, our sins no longer follow us and accuse us. As far as God is concerned, they're not there.

The resurrection of Jesus the Messiah changed everything for Cornelius the Roman centurion. He could love God with heart, soul, mind, and strength, and know Him intimately. He would still perform works of kindness, but those works would mean so much more.

3. Jesus as Lord means Jesus as judge.

Peter told Cornelius that Jesus was "appointed by God to be the Judge of the living and the dead" (Acts 10:42).

Many people don't like this side of Jesus. Friend and Savior is one thing—but Judge? That makes us nervous. Yet in order to be our Lord, He must be our judge. It's in the job description of a lord or master.

But here's the Good News: Jesus the judge is also Jesus the payment for sin. Imagine going before a judge in court, and the judge finds you guilty and assesses a fine that is far more than you could ever pay. But before you can protest, the judge goes over to the bailiff's table, pulls out his or her wallet, and pays the fine on your behalf. Christ our judge has paid the price for our sin.

4. Our belief is to be placed in Jesus Christ.

Peter said that forgiveness of our sins is tied to belief in Him.

Belief connects the dots—from His death and resurrection to the acceptance of His gift to the lordship He will now have in our lives. The Lord does *all* the work of salvation; the one thing required of us is belief.

What a glorious day when an entire Roman household was baptized into the family of God as followers of Jesus Christ. A representative of the soldiers who pierced His hands and feet now had his heart pierced by His love and lordship.

From Acts 1 through Acts 10, we have seen the unstoppable gospel moving out in shockwaves from the epicenter in

Jerusalem, to Judea and Samaria, and now to a handful of Roman citizens. And the shockwaves will continue to roll out to the ends of the earth.

Erasing the Dividing Line

Peter had brought Jewish believers with him (see v. 45). These Jewish Christians were astonished to see the Holy Spirit coming upon people who weren't Jewish and had never observed any of the important rituals. Peter wanted to know who would withhold the waters of baptism from people so clearly filled with the Holy Spirit. He was asked to stay for a few days, and we can imagine the fellowship they must have had, Jew to Roman.

Those "circumcised believers" had witnessed Pentecost. They'd seen Jewish Christians speaking in the languages of other people. In Acts 8, Peter and John had laid hands on the Samaritans (half-Jew, half-Gentile). Again the Holy Spirit had come. Now, in Acts 10, the circle is complete. The dots are all connected, and the picture is clear. People with no Jewish blood at all—Gentiles such as Cornelius—are included in that picture, and everyone declares the greatness of God.

Jews to half-Jews to non-Jews; Jerusalem to Judea and Samaria to the ends of the earth. Dot to dot to dot. It's a new line forming a new picture, and an old line has been erased—the dividing line between who can and can't come to God. The gospel is unstoppable. It pays no heed to any border humankind can draw. It recognizes no boundaries and it fears no obstacles. Even two thousand years later, the gospel is still knocking down walls and building bridges.

Years ago, I was in East Asia, riding in a taxicab with two other American pastors. We were on our way back to our hotel after a day of ministry, but we were caught in a traffic jam. I looked out my window and noticed a girl, about ten years old—delicate Asian features, dark hair, orange pants, and white T-shirt. She was jumping back and forth over a piece of concrete, singing, playing a child's game.

I thought, *If only I could communicate in her language! I'd get out of this car, go to her, and tell her about the love of the Savior.* But I couldn't. Yet that moment changed me. I realized the importance of sending more missionaries and mission teams. The view from my taxicab also watered the growing seed in my heart of how crucial a Mission 1:8 life is. Worshiping and listening from the pew is a blessing, but declaring and trusting in places of darkness is a priority.

Of course, I prayed that God would connect the dots and send someone to this little girl with the Good News. The traffic broke and so did my heart as we drove on. But I felt a new, stronger determination to push more stubbornly with the gospel. There are other dots, millions more dots, of every color, language, and nation. God was reminding me how much greater His picture is than just the United States. It's global, not just local. I had become so focused on my world that I forgot His world, and I desperately needed Him to recapture my attention.

Now, whenever I can, I give, go, and pray for the billions around the world who hunger for the Good News of Jesus Christ. Join me. I encourage you to go on a short-term mission trip with your church. I encourage you to give sacrificially to help spread the gospel around the world.

And I encourage you to dedicate yourself to Mission 1:8, to be the unstoppable connection of the Good News with the people around you, in your neighborhood, in your workplace, on your campus—wherever you are, wherever you go. Let God use you to connect the dots and complete the picture of His love for the world. This will connect things in your personal life too. The more we engage His global will, the more clearly we will see His will for us personally.

Take a step of faith and go. Take your kids with you. After all, many of us have taken our families to Disney World; I've done it a couple of times. We're led to believe that's what every good family does—we spend thousands of dollars to hear a few hundred dolls sing, "It's a small world after all."

Well, it's a big world—and it's a big thing to God that everyone hears about His love. If we can go to Disney World, why can't we also go into God's world with our families? Why can't we use a little vacation time to do something we'll never forget, something with eternal impact rather than entertainment value? It might be the best family decision you've ever made. It might just connect the dots for your kids, showing them what really matters in life. It might connect the dots in bringing all of you a closeness and a Spirit-filled love you've always wanted. Best of all, it might just connect the dots between Christ and someone far away who needs to hear about Him—someone He's sent your family to love and to bless.

What picture is the dots of your life putting together?

12

Prayer vs. Pride

The Difference between Freedom and Death

As I flew into Atlanta for a speaking engagement, it was a smooth flight until our final descent. I was enjoying that sense of coming out of the clouds and returning to the real world of streets and houses. But just seconds from touching down on the runway . . .

The plane tilted way too far.

As the left wing dipped toward the ground, my heart jumped into my throat. Then the right wing dipped, tossing the passengers sideways.

The engines roared to full throttle. The nose came up. We were shoved back against our seats as the plane lurched skyward. It was like riding a roller coaster—only the terror was real. The pilot had aborted our landing.

As we climbed higher, no one said a word. The plane circled around and retried the landing. This time, our touchdown was as smooth as silk.

What happened on the first attempt? Wake turbulence. As airplanes land, one after another, a large plane can stir up vortices of air, creating turbulence for the next aircraft in line.

Turbulence is an apt metaphor of what the church suffered in its early years. We'll see turbulence outside the church—persecution, martyrdom, imprisonment, and mob violence. And there will be turbulence within the church, including debates, discussions, and conflicts between believers. The more crises rocked the church, the more it grew.

Can we learn anything from them to help us with our own turbulent times?

Praying at Full Stride

After Saul's conversion, the threat of persecution subsided. Acts 9:31 tells us that the church grew during a time of peace. But it was short-lived.

King Herod attacked the church, executing James, the brother of John, by the sword. Tradition tells us that all the apostles other than John died as martyrs, but the death of James is the only one that Scripture confirms.

Peter was the next target, because he was the leader of the Jerusalem church. Insecure leaders are people pleasers, and Herod saw that the death of James went over well with his political supporters. The king imprisoned Peter with sixteen soldiers guarding him. He'd heard the rumors about Peter and John walking out of jail in the night, and he was taking no chances. After Passover, he would have Peter put to death.

Acts 12:5 tells us that the church prayed for Peter while he was imprisoned. This was no last resort for the church but rather a first priority. They knew they were talking to the One who created the universe, and that's no small thing.

Solomon observed, "The race is not to the swift, or the battle to the strong" (Eccles. 9:11). Sometimes the underdog wins.

Once, when I was in high school, I got a ticket I felt I didn't deserve. I went to the courthouse and defended myself in "The City of Houston v. Gregg Matte." That's what the summons called it, and as a teenager I was unnerved. The entire City of Houston versus me? A high school kid who sacked groceries after school for a living? But I got my day in court and won. Sometimes the little guy brings down the giant.

In Acts 12, a similar stage is set: King Herod versus Peter. Who will win? The king on his throne or the fisherman in chains?

The wild card in this confrontation is prayer. When you understand the reality of prayer, your perspective shifts. You realize that no one with God on his side is truly an underdog.

The church wasn't praying an anemic little "God bless Peter" prayer. Luke says the church prayed *earnestly* for Peter. The original Greek word Luke uses means that the church was praying "at full stride." Brisk, steady, like someone intent on getting where he's going. Do you pray at full stride?

The night before the trial, Peter slept between two soldiers. He didn't seem to have a care in the world. He had no idea what God might do; maybe he would be executed. He had faith, placed it all in his Lord's hands, and got a good night's sleep.

The resurrected Lord had prophesied to Peter that a time would come when "you will stretch out your hands and someone else will tie you and carry you where you don't want to go"

(John 21:18–19). Jesus was pointing to Peter's eventual death, and those words might have weighed on him right now—*This is just what Jesus said would happen.*

Instead of worrying, he slept, and an angel appeared. Peter was sleeping so peacefully that the angel had to punch him in the ribs to wake him up (see Acts 12:7). Light flooded the dark cell as the chains fell away from Peter. The angel gave him the plan: get dressed, wrap your cloak around you, and come on! Peter was apparently one of those people who doesn't function well before his coffee, and the angel had to hurry him along. Peter was thinking, *It's another vision. It's got to be.* There was a lot of that going around.

The angel led Peter into the street—and vanished. Peter had a heavenly parole, and he began to realize this was really happening. He also realized he could still make it to the prayer meeting occurring on his behalf; he could make quite the impression!

The girl who answered the door recognized his voice, lost her composure, and forgot to let him in. When she reported who was at the gate, everyone thought she'd lost her mind. But Peter was eventually admitted, there were probably quite a few hugs and high-fives, and Peter told his story.

Why are we so surprised when we get what we pray for? Peter's friends were shocked, and I imagine we'd have felt the same.

God invites us to pray—to take part in His movements on this planet. When we pray, "Your will be done on earth as it is in heaven," we're getting in on something eternal. Terrible things may happen. Evil may get the upper hand. But God's power always wins, and prayer gives us the chance to get in on the ground floor of that victory.

Little Guys and Big Prayers

This is basically the end of Peter's story in Acts, though we'll see him briefly one more time. And he goes out on a high note as an answered prayer.

I once visited a church in Cambridge, England. After a time of singing and greeting one another, the church prayed together. One gentleman in his seventies walked slowly to the front with the aid of a cane. Unable to stand for very long, he used his cane as a single-legged chair, sat down, and proceeded to pray. He prayed for a number of concerns, from the royal family to various needs in the church.

His voice grew stronger as he prayed, "Lord God, we stand against the evil that is coming against our children. We stand against the evil that is coming against our society. We stand in the power of Christ against the devil!" As this frail, elderly man thundered against evil, I peeked at him during the prayer and thought, *A mild gust of wind could knock him over, yet his prayers are battering the gates of hell.*

The early church was a bit like that man—weak, unsteady, standing against impossible odds. And it prayed with might and power, overcoming those odds. Prayer was the church's heartbeat, and it must be so again today. It must be so with individuals and with families. Do your children see you pray? Do you pray as a married couple? Do you have a prayer journal?

Pray on your knees to symbolize the posture of your heart. Some people think that's unnecessary, and they have a point. But we kneel because it humbles us and focuses us on receiving a message from God.

In 1999, I was the leader of Breakaway, a student ministry at Texas A&M. In the early morning hours of November 18, God woke me and placed a burden on my heart: *Pray for the campus.*

189

I climbed out of bed, got on my knees, and prayed for our school, even without a specific need. I told God that whatever it was, I would leave it in His hands. When I finished, I went back to bed.

A few hours later, one of my buddies called me and said, "Did you hear what happened?"

"No. What?"

He told me that fifty-eight students and former students had been working on the Aggie bonfire, assembling a stack of five thousand logs almost sixty feet high. The bonfire, a tradition since 1909, was part of our rivalry with the University of Texas at Austin.

Earlier that morning, at about 2:42 a.m., the log stack had collapsed. Twelve students were killed and twenty-seven injured. The rescue operation lasted more than twenty-four hours. Some of those students were in our ministry. I spent the day at the hospital, praying with students and family members.

If God wakes you up to pray for an urgent need, don't delay— go to your knees in prayer. You never know when you or someone close to you will encounter turbulence, and turbulent times call for earnest prayer.

Going Deeper with God

Prayer is more than a quick thanks for a meal or even a late-night wake-up call. Interacting with God must become interwoven with our lives rather than being some special event. Prayer is the true food of the soul, satisfying the hunger of the heart. A lack of prayer leaves us spiritually depleted, and in that situation we place our confidence in our own effort and derive our nourishment from our own skill. But prayer defers to Him, not ourselves. We were made to connect more profoundly than a series of yes and no questions for God.

Go deeper. Find *Him,* not simply personal direction. When your hunger for Him deepens, your ears will be open to His leading.

While on our trip to England, I took a cab ride in London. The cabbie was a Muslim who was fasting for Ramadan. I asked, "Why do you fast? What does fasting accomplish for you?"

"I really don't know," he said. "I'm just supposed to do it."

I said, "Fasting is something our faiths have in common. I believe in fasting as a Christian. But here's why I fast: most importantly, I want to know God better and hunger for Him more. I'm also fasting for God to do something in my life, and in our church. I'm asking for God to show up in a big way and do great things."

After sharing the gospel with him, I concluded, "I'm not fasting to earn a place in heaven. It's so that when the God of heaven speaks, I'll have ears to hear."

The Christians in Antioch had ears to hear when the Holy Spirit moved them to set apart Barnabas and Paul for the first missionary church. The people fasted, prayed, laid hands on them, and sent them off—an incredible moment in church history recorded for us in Acts 13. We notice that fasting is mentioned twice. It speaks of a desire to go deeper with God. Isn't that what we need in turbulent times? Spiritual depth is going to get us through. In verse 2, we read, "The Holy Spirit said." How many times does the Spirit speak with no one listening? Since the believers were praying and fasting, they had the knowledge of what God wanted them to do.

Many Christians have never considered fasting. They think it's weird, something for fanatics. Yet it's always had its place in God's will for us. If we're not sending and going and pushing for the gospel to spread, maybe it's because we're not fasting and listening and hearing from the Lord.

Let's be clear on what fasting is and is not. Fasting is *not* merely skipping a meal or two and going hungry in order to somehow punish our flesh. It's withdrawing from our normal routine in order that we may hear from heaven. Though we think of fasting as withdrawing from food, we can also fast by withdrawing from TV watching, the internet, or some other activity in order to devote more time to seeking the mind of God.

I've fasted on a certain day each week for a couple of years—not to be confused with the Daniel Fast I mentioned in chapter 2. Typically, I eat the evening meal one night, then skip breakfast and/or lunch the following day, then eat the evening meal the following night. I use the added time in my schedule to call out to God on behalf of our church.

A consistent commitment to fasting has truly changed my life.[1] I believe the discipline of fasting weekly has made me a more effective pastor and has impacted the ministry of our church in huge ways. I listen to God through fasting when our church needs to hire staff, or when I need guidance for Mission 1:8. I call out for power on Sunday, and He answers. I'm amazed by all God is doing, and I can trace it back to the growth of fasting and prayer in my life. Mission 1:8 became a movement, not just the latest fundraiser, because of a deeper hunger for God. The power of heaven is unlocked when we yearn for God in a place of sacrifice.

Here are some suggestions to help you to go deeper with God through fasting.

1. *Replace mealtime with prayer time.*

Don't simply skip a meal, replace that mealtime with work, and call it fasting. This is about more prayer. If you normally eat for thirty minutes, then pray for thirty minutes.

2. *Replace the hunger of your stomach with a hunger of your heart.*

We're more than physical beings and we hunger for more than food. I try to use my physical hunger to stimulate my spiritual appetite. Whenever I feel a twinge of physical hunger, I pray, "Lord, I'm hungry—but I have a deeper hunger to hear your voice. I'm hungry for you to work in my life. I'm hungry for your power." Every twinge of physical hunger reminds me of my heart's *true* hunger.

3. *Replace willpower with God's power.*

Hunger is temptation during fasting. We tend to "gut it out" and will our way through. But we're interested in spiritual disciplines, not physical ones. Call out to God for the strength to maintain your discipline of fasting. Ask Him to teach you faithfulness, and to let His strength fill your weakness.

Pick your time, take the step, and you'll feel blessed. God will move, speak, and send.

Two Forms of Pride

If you're extra-resistant to fasting, check your pride quotient. It's the natural deterrent to anything that draws us closer to God—particularly fasting.

193

I once heard of a brilliant door-to-door salesman who closed hundreds of sales by saying, "A lot of your neighbors told me you couldn't afford our product, but I thought they were wrong." Few people can resist a direct towel-snap to their pride!

Of all the sins we're prone to, pride scares me the most. Part of the problem is that there's a good pride. It's the kind that looks back with satisfaction. You've worked hard and done something well, and it's natural to feel good about that. We're proud of how far we've come; we're proud of our families. We want our children to take pride in their schoolwork and accomplishments.

Healthy pride features gratitude to God. Like Olympic sprinter Eric Liddell in *Chariots of Fire*, we feel God's pleasure when we do our thing. Why shouldn't we enjoy that?

But that form of pride has an evil twin—and it's consumed by insecurity. Sinful pride wants to impress other people. It's hungry for fame, glory, and status. It doesn't compete with others in a healthy way—it wants to crush the competition. Others must decrease so that it can increase. That's how people are when we're filled with sinful pride. We'll let you know how great we are, because we fear it's just the opposite.

Acts 12:21–24 tells an interesting story of King Herod Agrippa I. Like many leaders, he was as insecure as he was powerful. One day, Luke tells us, Herod was dressed in his royal robes and seated on a throne on the stage of an outdoor theater in Caesarea. He was preparing to deliver a speech before the people.

The historian Josephus, in *Antiquities of the Jews*, recounts this same event. Josephus tells us that the royal robe Agrippa wore was "made wholly of silver" (that is, it was woven of silver threads—bling like you've never seen before). The morning sun hit the silver filaments and made them sparkle. The people hailed Agrippa as a god. The assembled people began to shout, "It's the voice of a god and not of a man!" (v. 22).

And the king didn't correct them. If they thought he was a god, who was he to disagree? He wore silver to steal the glory of the sun—or, in this case, the Son.

Luke and Josephus both agree that God's judgment was swift. An angel struck the king for his refusal to give God the glory. Agrippa was infected with worms and died (v. 23).

Josephus is regarded as the most reliable of historians. He wrote from a Jewish but not a Christian perspective. His agreement with Luke verifies that Acts, too, can be trusted in its historical details.

Five Steps to the Grave

"Pride comes before destruction, and an arrogant spirit before a fall" (Prov. 16:18). Agrippa should have studied that verse. He followed five steps to the grave.

Step 1: Private pride can lead to a public fall.

Public arrogance always begins with a tiny seed of pride within the heart. Before Agrippa ordered his robe of silver threads, some insecure part of him said, *I need more praise. I need to hear the people tell me I'm a god.* That's where it began—in the private recesses of his needy heart.

I hate to tell the following story—it hurts my pride! I was an intern youth minister in DeSoto, Texas, near Dallas. Every summer we took our youth group to the Youth Evangelism Conference, a gathering of thousands of students. One time, I looked up at the stage and the thought hit me: *Someday, I'm going to speak from that stage.* That thought came straight from my prideful hunger for attention, not a desire to impact students.

There was a man on the stage performing feats of strength. He would shatter bricks and bend steel bars with his bare hands, then make a spiritual application. He pointed to a towel on a chair near where I sat. He said, "Would someone bring that towel to me, please?"

I reached out and grabbed it, thinking, *This is my moment! I'll be up on that stage!* Someone else also reached for the towel, but I had a better grip and snatched it away. Then I hopped up on the stage and handed the towel to the man.

Returning to my seat, I saw one of the kids in our youth group directly in front of me. He was a bit of a troubled kid, and I had been trying to reach out to him. But I saw him eyeing me with disgust. "Dude," he said, "that was cold."

Then I saw it: I'd yanked that towel away from a ten-year-old boy. He was standing by his mother, crying, and his mother was looking daggers at me. I felt three inches tall.

I had blown it with everybody. And I mean *everybody.* Our images had been on the Jumbotron, up close and personal. Pride in vivid detail.

I went and apologized to the boy and his mom. The boy accepted my apology. The mom—not so much.

As I sat there, marinating in self-reproach, I asked myself, *Why did I do that?*

Pride is a little seed that suddenly takes Jumbotron proportions, once we see what it's all about. It starts with a secret thought: *Someday, I'm going to speak from that stage.* (By the way, I've never been invited to speak there.)

196

Step 2: Pride always lifts up the wrong god.

When the people shouted that Herod was a god, not a man, he wallowed in the applause. He became a tinfoil god.

Some people have been told by a parent or boss, "You'll never amount to anything." People who hear such destructive messages often set up a false god of success to bolster their pride. They're terrified the prophecy will come true, and they devote their lives to proving it wrong.

Idolatry is putting anything or anyone other than the one true God on the throne. When we exalt Jesus as God, humility happens.

A Christian college professor once told me, "Whenever you feel the temptation to be prideful, tell yourself, 'No pride, just joy.'" Those words have become a constant refrain in my life. I don't want pride in my life, because pride brings a fall. I just want joy—the joy of knowing Jesus as my Lord and my God, and the joy of celebrating His blessings. No pride, just joy.

Step 3: Pride negates the soul and elevates the flesh.

Herod was all about the bling rather than what's on the inside. Our flesh is vain, lazy, selfish, boastful, lustful, envious of others, hypocritical, and easily provoked. The flesh says, "It's all about me." We're never content; we always want more and always covet what others have. While the godly soul wants to influence others and glorify God, the flesh wants to impress others and glorify itself.

As Jesus said to His disciples, if we seek the flesh we will lose our souls, but if we will crucify the flesh we'll give life to our souls. Jesus said we must deny ourselves, take up our crosses—which is the opposite of pride—and follow Him. For what good is it to gain the whole world and lose your soul (see Matt. 16:24–26)?

Herod Agrippa makes a great illustration of that. At the exact moment he gained the whole world, his life was over—lost. And he had nothing to give in exchange for his life.

Benjamin Franklin put it this way in his autobiography:

> There is, perhaps, no one of our natural passions so hard to subdue as pride. Disguise it, struggle with it, beat it down, stifle it, mortify it as much as one pleases, it is still alive, and will every now and then peep out and show itself . . . for, even if I could conceive that I had completely overcome it, I should probably be proud of my humility.[2]

Step 4: Pride limits our eternal purpose and the flourishing of the gospel.

After God struck Herod Agrippa down and vanquished his pride, Luke writes, "God's message flourished and multiplied" (Acts 12:24). Once the prideful man was out of the picture, God's message went forth.

Humility advances our ministry. Pride impedes the work of God. God is patient, and wants us to come to repentance, but He will not permit us to thwart His will forever. Our pride sets us at odds with God. C. S. Lewis said that as long as we're proud, we can't know God, for "a proud man is always looking down on things and people: and, of course, as long as you are looking down, you cannot see something that is above you."[3]

I am proud of our church, Houston's First Baptist Church— but I pray we never become a proud church. As believers, we should have a healthy pride in doing the work God has given us to do. But may we never become prideful and say, "Look at what we have done!" We should be humbled by experiencing God's greatness as He uses us. And when we are humble, the gospel will flourish.

Step 5: Pride brings death.

The king died of pride, and it was an ugly way to go.

I used to picture this man's death as a scene from the movie *Alien*. I imagined Herod was speaking to the crowd when worms suddenly burst from him and he died screaming. But Josephus tells us Agrippa didn't get off that easy. He suffered for five days. Pride is a slow killer, a worm that eats you from the inside out.

Pride will kill you by killing your marriage, your family, your friendships, and your work. There's nothing it won't consume. A well-known poem by William Ernest Henley, "Invictus," is a statement of pride:

> Out of the night that covers me,
> Black as the pit from pole to pole,
> I thank whatever gods may be
> For my unconquerable soul.
> In the fell clutch of circumstance
> I have not winced nor cried aloud.
> Under the bludgeonings of chance
> My head is bloody, but unbowed. . . .
> It matters not how strait the gate,
> How charged with punishments the scroll,
> *I am the master of my fate,*
> *I am the captain of my soul.*[4]

Herod Agrippa could have quoted those words, for they say, "I have no need of a savior." What will the end of your life be if you say, "I don't need Jesus. I am the master of my fate and the captain of my soul"?

God will say to you, "I wish you had chosen differently, but I allowed you to choose. Your pride has bought you separation from Me for all eternity. *Your* will be done."

In the epic battle between Peter the fisherman and Herod the king, who won? One chose prayer, the other pride. Peter slept to be awakened to an angel and freedom. Herod slept to awaken to demons. The man in prison did better than the king with the silver sheen.

Pride brings death; prayer and fasting bring freedom. In turbulent times, we humble ourselves and pray. And the results are very predictable: no pride, just joy.

13

Unstoppable Impact

Four Groups to Touch Forever

A few years ago, my wife and I were on a mission trip to Hong Kong. Walking down the street, we saw a man on the sidewalk wearing a black T-shirt with lettering that read, "In My World, You Don't Exist."

That's kind of rude, I said to myself. Then, with a jolt: *But isn't that how I often treat others? Sometimes I'm so set on checking off my "to-dos" that I don't even see the people around me.*

Unless we live on a five-foot by five-foot island, we all deal with a number of people. How do we see them? As eternal human souls? As the walking wounded who need a healing touch? Or do they simply not exist in our world?

Let's see how Paul the apostle did it.

In Acts 17:16, we find Paul sitting in Athens, waiting for his companions. Everywhere he looked he found idol worship, and it broke his heart. In Athens alone, we know there were as many as three thousand public statues and thirty thousand idols. In *The Satyricon*, Roman satirist Petronius Arbiter, who lived at that time, said it was easier to find a god than a man in that city.[1]

Athens was the intellectual center of the world—and a place of idolatry and superstition. There were shrines and statues to Greek gods at the front door of every house, around the marketplace, and even at street crossings. As Plato wrote in *Timaeus*, "All men who have any right feeling, at the beginning of any enterprise, call upon the gods."[2]

It was probably Paul's first experience in an idol-drenched culture. So many gods, and the one true God not even represented!

Paul had a rough exterior with a caring heart. He is a great example for you and me; we need his deep love for lost people. A phrase I've thought of many times to make it as a pastor is, "Thick skin, soft heart." And that's the picture of Paul.

Lucy, of "Peanuts" comic strip fame, said, "I love mankind. It's people I can't stand." Some of us have warm, fuzzy feelings about humanity, as long as the humanity is across the ocean somewhere. It's the real people in our little circle—the rude co-workers, the neighbors with the shaggy lawns—that we write off. Clue: God loves them all, near and far.

We need to be able to let our eyes fall on the people in close proximity, as Paul did, and realize that God placed us right here, right now, to be compassionate 1:8 missionaries.

The Four People You Meet in the Marketplace

Paul had a clear strategy he used time and again: roll into town, start in the synagogue, then walk into the *agora*, the marketplace, and spark some conversation.

So he reasoned in the synagogue with the Jews and with those who worshiped God and in the marketplace every day with those who happened to be there. Then also, some of the Epicurean and Stoic philosophers argued with him. Some said, "What is this pseudo-intellectual trying to say?"

Others replied, "He seems to be a preacher of foreign deities"—because he was telling the good news about Jesus and the Resurrection. (Acts 17:17–18)

Paul encountered these four groups:

1. The potential: Jews and those who worshiped God
2. The passersby: those who happened to be in the marketplace
3. The pleasure-seekers: Epicurean philosophers
4. The prideful: Stoic philosophers

Do you think those are exotic, defunct groups from ancient times? Think again.

Group 1: The potential.

According to the Gallup polling organization, 92 percent of Americans believe in God.[3] But how many Americans truly have trusted in Jesus Christ as Lord and Savior? I don't know—but I guarantee it's less than 92 percent!

Paul always fished first where they'd been biting in the past. The Jews didn't know Christ but they knew God, if only through a works-based religion. Paul could use the ancient prophecies, and his audience could follow his reasoning.

Don't you know people who "do" a certain amount of religion without experiencing it at soul-level? Maybe they show up at church once per year. Jesus is "just all right" with them, but they can't say they know Him well.

Like Paul, we have a foundation to build on with these folks. They identify with Christianity, so they'll talk with you about it. They don't hate our faith; they're just lukewarm and probably craving something deeper, whether they know it or not. There's *potential*—but it needs to become reality. These people need to come to know Christ intimately, to trust Him as true Lord and not someone who makes an annual appearance in their thinking. He died for them; it's time for them to live for Him.

Many of "the potential" are either confused or have never heard a clear presentation of the gospel. They have the bare basics, but probably have no idea what they're missing—eating moldy crackers when a gourmet meal is within reach. That was me as a teen. I wanted to please and know God. I just didn't know how. I needed someone to care enough to befriend me and show me the Way, the Truth, and the Life.

Group 2: The passersby.

There were always people in the marketplace of Athens— just as there are always people with whom we rub shoulders in everyday life. Consider three categories.[4]

- *Scenery*. Most of the passersby we see fade into the backdrop. Cars on the freeway; shoppers ahead of us in line; in general, people in our way. We don't see them as human souls in need of Christ. And yet they are.
- *Machinery*. Some people are necessary to us: flight attendants, baristas, clerks, waiters. They're the machinery of our lives, performing essential functions—and that's how we see them, just nuts and bolts. We focus on what we need rather than what they need. And they need Christ.

- *Ministry.* How large is this category through your eyes? Can you see everyday people as eternal souls? People are not scenery or machinery but lost children of God's kingdom. Our interactions can be divinely appointed intersections. Will we pass them by or will we find ways to bless them?

Once, while I was in New Orleans to speak, some friends and I went to Café Du Monde in the French Quarter for beignets and coffee. As we were leaving, I noticed our waitress and another waitress sitting near the entrance on a break. God impressed upon me, *Your waitress is your ministry, not just machinery.* I felt a brief tug of resistance—*I'll pray silently for her.* But I knew God wanted me to talk to her.

So I went to her and said, "Thank you for helping us today. I'm a Christian. Is there anything I can pray about for you? Maybe someone in your family I can pray for?"

Both of these waitresses were Vietnamese immigrants and the language barrier was a problem, but with effort, we communicated. It turned out that they were sisters. When my waitress understood what I was saying, tears welled in her eyes. Her sister said, "You pray for her. Everything wrong in her life."

She could have been just machinery when she waited on us, just scenery as I passed by on the way out. But what God wanted was ministry.

Group 3: The pleasure seekers.

The Epicureans were all about the right *feelings*. Epicurus, the founder of this system, had no interest in gods or goodness. He was after freedom from fear or pain. Today's pleasure seekers live by the mantra, "You only live once." Since this life is all there is, there's no higher purpose to life than pleasure. Just have a good time while it lasts.

Paul came talking of sin and salvation, and pleasing God rather than self. As a result, he was mocked and called a pseudo-intellectual, which literally means "seed picker" in the term they used—someone who picks up scraps. They couldn't have been more condescending.

Unlike the potential believers, the pleasure seekers had no background in the Scriptures. Paul had to start with the basics, explaining the existence of God and the problem of sin. Why would they care that Jesus paid for their sins if they didn't know they even had any sins?

Increasingly we encounter people with no foundation in spiritual understanding. They don't understand why they need to be saved, or even acknowledge there is a God. So we have to go back to the basics of a Creator who loves them and wants a relationship, even if they mock us. At some point, our descriptions of a futile life without God and an abundant life with Him will hit home, and they'll begin to feel deep conviction in the soul they didn't know they had—prayerfully and hopefully turning their hearts to Jesus.

Group 4: The prideful.

The Stoics believed they could eliminate suffering through intellectual perfection (a state they called *apatheia*, "without passion"). They just needed to do more thinking. Who needed a Savior when all the answers were inside their heads?

We recognize modern Stoics easily enough. They're people who are the captains of their own souls and they need no crew, no navigation devices. And life is smooth sailing until they run into an iceberg.

We all face crises we simply can't handle on our own, and that's the moment when all our arrogant preconceptions tumble. It's a humbling experience. When we encounter people who are realizing they're inadequate to face the great problems of life, we need to be gentle, forgiving, and helpful. Jesus offered compassion and healing to people like that, and so should we.

	Who	How
1.	Potential	Pray: Their eyes would be opened to something more
		Discuss: Christianity is relationship, not rules
2.	Passersby	Pray: For opportunities and intersections
		Discuss: Prayer, care, and share
3.	Pleasure Seekers	Pray: They would be dissatisfied with the world
		Discuss: There's more to life
4.	Prideful	Pray: For brokenness
		Discuss: Human insufficiency and offers of care when life crashes

Heart Cultivation

In Acts 17, Paul shows us three principles to cultivate a heart that cares for the potential believers, the passersby, the pleasure seekers, and the prideful people.

Principle 1: Slow down and notice.

Paul must have been restless. He was a type-A personality, but he had to get the lay of the land before he sprang into action. So he became a people watcher. Acts 17:16 says, "While Paul was *waiting* . . . he *saw*" (emphasis added). Watching people not only helped him understand them but care deeply about them. Have you noticed how that works?

Once we look past the machinery and the scenery and put aside our hectic agendas for a few minutes, we start to identify with people. That waitress who brought you the wrong meal, it turns out, has a lot of problems on her mind. Suddenly you don't care about the burger she brought you; you want to encourage her.

How many of us not-so-good Samaritans walk right by people with whom we might have made a difference, just because we were in a hurry to get to something ultimately less important? The disciples wanted to push through the crowd and sweep those annoying little children aside, but Jesus said, "Let them come." He had the most important agenda in history but it didn't stop Him from braking for children and other needy people.

It's right to care about tsunamis and hurricanes across the world, but there are emotional disasters going on all around us. That angry person in your office is, in all probability, a hurting person, not an evil one who set out to annoy you. What an opportunity you have.

Do you want to be more caring? Start by simply opening your eyes. Stop, look, and listen to what is going on around you. Read between the lines. Where are the hurts? And as for all those busy items on the to-do list—God has a way of taking care of them when we do His work.

Principle 2: Sin should break us, not entertain us.

If Paul had been like most of us, he might have said, "Greece is so cool! All these lovely idols. Note to self: must tour the false god statue factory."

Paul wasn't entertained by colorful Athens—he was depressed and disturbed. He saw sin. He looked through the eyes of Jesus and saw demonic deception and false philosophies.

As Christians, we shouldn't spend our dollars to be "entertained" by content that pollutes our minds and damages our souls. We are surrounded by idolatry, moral pollution, perversion, and false religion packaged as "entertainment." Instead of being entertained by sin, let's walk in step with Christ, speaking the Good News as Paul did. We have something better to fill our eyes and mind with and something far better to offer. We have the unstoppable gospel.

Principle 3: Show up.

Paul could have chosen to hang out at the synagogue or hole up in his room at the Athens Hilton. Instead, he went to the marketplace where the people were, and he struck up conversations. He had the get-up-and-go, so he got up and went.

Paul never simply let things happen. He took the initiative. Back when he thought Christians were dangerous heretics, he tried to do something about it. When he found he had it wrong, and Christianity was the hope of the world, he did something about that. Once he showed up and checked in, God always had a job for him. He will for you too.

Christian women in our city were burdened about local sex workers—prostitutes, escorts, erotic dancers, and so forth. So these concerned women went to where it all happened (during daylight hours, taking precautions to be safe). There they would pray, and often they went into the clubs and befriended the women who worked there.

They'd say, "We want to bring you some gifts to show you we care about you." Their new friends were genuinely moved. The cashier in a so-called gentlemen's club was pregnant, so our ladies held a baby shower for her. Read this amazing email one of our ladies sent me:

I prayed all week about the perfect shower gift. I felt the Lord telling me to give her a Bible. But doubts flooded my mind: *She'll probably get lots of Bibles. I should give her something practical like baby clothes.* In the end, I ignored the doubts and bought her a lovely leather Bible.

The ladies arranged a beautiful party, with flowers, tea, sandwiches, cake, and gifts. The mother-to-be was overwhelmed. As she unwrapped my gift, I was nervous—but then her face lit up and she whispered, "This is my first Bible!"

She was thirty-eight years old, and had never owned a Bible. If I had listened to my doubts, I would have missed the joy of giving the most precious gift, God's Word.

Something beautiful happened because these women *showed up* and let God do the rest. This is when the church shines before the world. Think about it: a group of church ladies gives a baby shower for an unmarried pregnant woman who works in a seedy gentlemen's club?

A church of impact is made up of people of impact. If you want to have an impact on potential believers, passersby, pleasure seekers, and prideful people, ask God to give you a spirit that is sensitive to needs. Don't worry about your gifts or eloquence. Just do it. Go in the name of Jesus. Show up and shine.

And while you're at it, read over those four categories one more time. As you do so, ask God to bring people to mind who fit them—people from your circles. Let God know you're ready to show up.

Students, senior adults, businesspeople—the beauty of it is that everyone has a different kind of circle, and you're the best-equipped person in the world to make a difference in your circle.

Point A to Point B via Point Z

On September 1, 1939, the Second World War began as the Nazis invaded Poland. Great Britain launched Operation Pied Piper, an effort to move 3.5 million children out of harm's way. The bombers were coming soon, so it was important to get the little ones out of the cities and into the countryside.

The story is told of a boy standing in a London train station, tears in his eyes, a destination tag attached to his clothing. A man walked up and said, "Son, do you know where you're going?"

"No, but the king does."

Paul had that mindset near the end of his second missionary journey. It had been war up to then—attacks, setbacks, opposition. Yet he knew the King had a plan and was sending him where he needed to be. The church was on mission as the King of kings led them from the epicenter of Jerusalem to the ends of the earth, from Jews to Gentiles, from Saul to Paul, from East to West.

The story hurries on. Acts 18 and 19 take us through Paul's third missionary journey, building and strengthening churches in many cities; and then to Ephesus, where he lived for almost three years, preaching Christ and directing church growth all around.

Near the end of his time in Ephesus, Paul resolved in the Spirit to follow an itinerary that would lead him to Jerusalem—and then Rome (see Acts 19:21). He took a roundabout route because he wanted to collect donations from the Greek churches to help during a terrible crisis among the believers in Jerusalem. He describes it in his own words in Romans 15:25–31. He was willing to go out of his way to follow God's leading.

Sometimes we prize efficiency—or our perception of it— more than God does. If we take things into our own hands, trying to be brisk and competent, we miss the holy serendipity of the ways God wants to do things. It wasn't "efficient" for God to send His Son through Bethlehem and give Him only three years to minister—but that way glorified God. He didn't need six days to create the universe; He could have done it in one moment. But He is more than a heavenly production manager. He is an Artist. And sometimes His most beautiful work is found in times and places and methods we'd never have planned.

Paul heard the Spirit's leading, and it may have seemed like a zig-zag way to go—from point A to B by way of Z—but he was obedient.

It's wonderful that we're using our minds and our creativity for God's kingdom, but if we forget to use His leading, we're defeated before we begin. He doesn't need our efficiency or planning; He desires our availability and simple obedience.

I would never have planned my life the way it has worked out, but what blessings He has given me. I trust it's the same for you. His ways are not our ways. "A man's heart plans his way, but the LORD determines his steps" (Prov. 16:9).

Life surprises us all. Sometimes we are surprised by joy, sometimes we are stunned by affliction. But God calls us to trust Him and follow where He leads. And when people ask, "Do you know where you're going?" we answer, "No, but the King does."

Unstoppable!

Paul indeed reached Rome, and there he awaited trial. Like they had been with Jesus and Peter and Stephen, the predictable accusers were ready with their trumped-up charges. And the book of Acts ends with something of a cliffhanger. Is Paul acquitted or is he found guilty? Perhaps the point is that, for God's purposes, the accusers can't win. In the end, they are the ones who will stand trial before Him. Luke has told us enough of a story to allow us to know that the church is unstoppable, regardless of Paul's trial. Acts concludes with Paul under house arrest, welcoming visitors and preaching the gospel.

> Then he stayed two whole years in his own rented house. And he welcomed all who visited him, proclaiming the kingdom of God and teaching the things concerning the Lord Jesus Christ with full boldness and *without hindrance*. (Acts 28:30–31, emphasis added)

The book opens with a handful of terrified disciples. It closes with Paul, ambassador for Christ par excellence, telling the story of Jesus "without hindrance" in the capital of the known world. History will continue, and each day will bring fresh attempts to silence the followers of Jesus. And the gospel will continue to prove unstoppable.

The acts of the Holy Spirit through the followers of Jesus continue, and perhaps the most exciting pages are yet to be written in your lifetime and in mine, in your church and mine, in our neighborhoods, and across the globe.

Mission 1:8 is our sacred charge. Onward in God's unstoppable power for His unstoppable gospel!

But you will receive power when the Holy Spirit has come on you, and you will be My witnesses in Jerusalem, in all Judea and Samaria, and to the ends of the earth. (Acts 1:8)

Appendix 1

Taking the Next Step in Prayer

We all want to be prayerful but sometimes need help knowing how. In this appendix I want to help you take the next step in your prayer life.

First Things First

If you don't know where to start, you can pray by following this acrostic:

Praise: Thank God for who He is.
Repentance: Confess your sins and need for His strength.
Ask: Submit you requests to Him.
Yield: Declare your heart to follow Him.[1]

The Daniel Fast

On my Daniel Fast, I was praying for the next ten years of my family and ministry. Each day had a different request for each person, for the next ten years. Many of my prayers for my kids were based on their ages. Here's how I organized the prayer requests:

Ten-Day Daniel Fast Prayer Chart

I am fasting for ____(My child's name)_____

Day of Fast	Calendar Year	Person's Age	Prayer Request
1	(This year)	(Current age)	
2	(Next year)	(Current age +1)	
3			
4			
5			
6			
7			
8			
9			
10			

Examples of what I prayed for on each day:

- **My son**: high school selection, friends, purity, faith, college selection, life's calling, ministry impact, godliness, marriage, and wife-to-be.
- **My daughter**: find love and value in Christ, the right role models, self-esteem and beauty in Christ, quiet times, boys and purity, friends and activities.
- **My wife**: growth, wisdom, mind to dwell on truth, peace, strong friendships, and faith.

- **My church**: reach the lost, missions heart, strong staff, biblical teaching, raise up leaders, worldwide influence, protection morally and physically, discipleship, and pastoral succession (I have no plans to leave, but one day someone else will sit in my chair).
- **Myself**: this book you are reading, friendships, wisdom, leadership, humility, creativity, passion for my calling, to live for eternal rewards, my heart, and God's plan for my life.

A Daniel Fast can be difficult. Here are a few books that helped us:

- *The Daniel Fast: Feed Your Soul, Strengthen Your Spirit, and Renew Your Body* by Susan Gregory (Tyndale, 2010)
- *The Power of Prayer and Fasting*, second edition, by Ronnie Floyd (B&H, 2010)
- The Book of Daniel in the Bible would also obviously be good to read.

Mission 1:8 Ministries

Our church's journey of Mission 1:8 has been incredible. The unstoppable gospel has been released through our generosity to reach our city, nation, and world, and to remember the poor, widow, prisoner, and orphan.

Below is a list of the ministries Houston's First Baptist Church has partnered with financially and prayerfully as we live out Mission 1:8. Thankfully we are continuing to add to this list. I encourage you to google any that pique your interest to find out more information.

Our City

Houston's First Cypress Campus
Houston's First Downtown Campus
Houston's First Sienna Campus
Houston's First Spanish Campus

Many of the ministries in the "Poor, Widow, Prisoner, and Orphan" section minister in our city as well.

Our Nation

Calvary Baptist Church, SBC Pastors Conference
City On A Hill Church (Brookline, MA)
Embark Church (Worcester, MA)
Epic Church (San Francisco, CA)
First Baptist Church (New York, NY)
Metropolitan New York Baptist Association (eighteen church plants)

Mill City Church (Lowell, MA)
NETS (New England)
North American Mission Board
Redeemer Fellowship Church (Watertown, MA)
The Bridge Church (Brooklyn, NY)
The Journey Church (Staten Island, NY)
The Movement Church (Oakland, CA)

Our World

Cana Family Life (Kenya)
Comunidade Batista Oceanica (Rio de Janeiro, Brazil)
Encounter Church (Sherbrooke, Quebec)
Equip Worship
Feeding Events (India)
House Church Leader Conferences (East Asia)
Iglesia Evangélica Bautista (Xátiva, Spain)
Immanuel Baptist Church (Madrid, Spain)
International Mission Board
J-People (Unreached People Group)
La Chapelle church plant (Montreal, Quebec)
Manoto Archie (Cambodia)
Parklands Baptist Church (Kenya)
Ridgeways Baptist Church (Kenya)
Spring Valley School (Southern India)
T-People (Unreached People Group)
Wycliffe Bible Translation

Poor, Widow, Prisoner, and Orphan

As Our Own (India)
Association of Christian Orphanages of Guatemala
Back2Back Ministries (Mexico)

C.H.A.R.M. Prison Ministries
CLAY Student Leadership
Cornerstone Family Ministries
Eagles Nest (East Asia)
Empowered to Connect (various countries)
Every Village (South Sudan)
Family Legacy Missions International
Free Indeed Ministries
Generation One
Hearts for Ghana Mission
His Cherished Ones (Kenya)
His Voice Global (South Sudan)
Hope for Youth
Houston Habitat for Humanity
Houston Pregnancy Center
Into Abba's Arms (Kenya)
LifeHouse of Houston
Lifesong for Orphans
Living Water International (various countries)
Maasai Tribe (Kenya)
Mike Eden Ministries (Kenya)
Mission Centers of Houston
Mission: Dignity (Guidestone)
Montrose Street Reach
Northrise University (Zambia)
Open Door Mission
Romanian Christian Enterprises
Southwestern Baptist Theological Seminary, Darrington Unit
Star of Hope Mission
The Forge for Families
The Harbor (Russia)
The Source for Women
Village of Hope (Guatemala)
WorkFaith Connection
Youth Reach

Notes

Introduction

1. Mark Galli, "Andrew Sullivan Says Forget the Church; That's Like Saying Forget Grace," *Christianity Today*, April 17, 2012, http://www.christianitytoday.com/ct/2012/aprilweb-only/sullivan-forget-church.html.

Chapter 1 Mission in Motion

1. Lisa Kepner, "Yates, Ira Griffith, Jr.," *Texas State Historical Association*, June 15, 2010, http://www.tshaonline.org/handbook/online/articles/fyazp; Thomas L. Friedman, "Yates Field in Texas Is Key to Deal," *New York Times*, November 20, 1981, http://www.nytimes.com/1981/11/20/business/yates-field-in-texas-is-key-to-deal.html; "Ira Griffith Yates," *Connectville*, http://wc.rootsweb.ancestry.com/cgi-bin/igm.cgi?op=GET&db=connectville&id=I15511.

2. Charles Caldwell Ryrie, *The Acts of the Apostles* (Chicago: Moody, 1961), Kindle edition.

3. Luke is widely believed to have been a Greek physician born in Syrian Antioch, and was converted to Christianity by Paul. Some scholars, however, think he may have been a Grecian Jew. Paul, in Colossians 4:14, calls him "the dearly loved physician."

4. Terry C. Muck, *Those Other Religions in Your Neighborhood* (Grand Rapids: Zondervan, 1992), 150–51.

5. See appendix 2 for a list of ministries Mission 1:8 has supported.

6. Abby Stocker, "The Craziest Statistic You'll Read About North American Missions," *Christianity Today*, August 19, 2013.

7. Abe C. Van Der Puy, "What They Said About World Evangelism," Bible.org, February 2, 2009, https://bible.org/illustration/what-they-said-about-world-evangelism.

8. Ibid.

Chapter 2 The Power Line

1. Mary Ann Bridgwater heads our pre-service prayer time at Houston's First Baptist; resources can be found at www.praytheword.org.

2. Corrie McKee, "Asian Students Tear Down Walls," *Urbana Today*, December 31, 2009, 6.

3. Phillips Brooks, "Going up to Jerusalem," *Twenty Sermons* (New York: Dutton, 1886), 330.

Chapter 3 Going Global

1. "How many spoken languages are there in the world?" *Infoplease*, January 17, 2015, http://www.infoplease.com/askeds/many-spoken-languages.html.

Chapter 4 All Roads to the Cross

1. John Maxwell, *Everyone Communicates, Few Connect: What the Most Effective People Do Differently* (Nashville: Thomas Nelson, 2010), 205.

2. Lee Eclov, "Blasphemy!" *Preaching Today*, January 19, 2015, http://www.preachingtoday.com/sermons/sermons/2006/january/searchingthesoul4.html.

Chapter 5 Love in Three Words

1. Andrew Murray, *The State of the Church: An Urgent Call to Repentance and Prayer*, contemporized ed. (Fort Washington, PA: CLC Publications, 1983), 71.

2. Ed Stetzer, "Preach the Gospel, and Since It's Necessary, Use Words," *Tabletalk*, June 12, 2012.

Chapter 6 For Us, Not from Us

1. Dorothy Kelley Patterson and Rhonda Harrington Kelley, eds., *Women's Evangelical Commentary: New Testament* (Nashville: B&H, 2011), 273.

2. Julie Bullock of Generis helped to guide us along. She did a great job. More information at www.generis.com.

3. Nelson Searcy with Jennifer Dykes Henson, *Maximize: How to Develop Extravagant Givers in Your Church* (Grand Rapids, MI: Baker, 2010), 204.

4. I first heard this idea presented by Andy Stanley as a "*tension* to be managed instead of a problem to be solved" in a leadership podcast, "The Upside of Tension," Catalyst 2014.

5. See Matthew 26:9.

6. J. Rendel Harris, ed. and trans., *The Apology of Aristides: On Behalf of the Christians: Contributions to Biblical and Patristic Literature, Texts and*

Studies, vol. 1 (Eugene, OR: Wipf and Stock, 2004), 48–49.

Chapter 7 At the Corner of Now and Eternity

1. Brian Mains, "Marion Shurtleff makes amazing discovery in used Bible, finds childhood essay she wrote 65 years ago," *WCPO Digital*, June 28, 2013, http://www.wcpo.com/news/marion-shurtleff-makes-amazing-discovery-in-used-bible-finds-childhood-essay-she-wrote-65-years-ago.

Chapter 8 Courageous at the Flashpoint

1. Robert J. Morgan, *Nelson's Complete Book of Stories, Illustrations, and Quotes* (Nashville: Thomas Nelson, 2000), ebook edition.

2. Harper Lee, *To Kill a Mockingbird* (New York: Hachette, 1982), 149.

3. Jim Forsyth, "Federal Appeals Court Opens Doors for Prayer at Texas Graduation," *Reuters*, June 3, 2011, http://www.reuters.com/article/2011/06/04/us-graduation-prayer-texas-idUSTRE75300O20110604.

4. Arek Sarkissian II, "Port Wentworth Nixes Prayer at Senior Center," *Savannah Morning News*, May 7, 2010, http://savannahnow.com/news/2010-05-08/port-wentworth-nixes-prayer-senior-center.

5. Dave Tombers, "Social Worker Bans Religious Conversation," *World Net Daily*, October 23, 2012, http://www.wnd.com/2012/10/social-worker-bans-religious-conversation/.

6. Rob Kerby, "Federal Cemetery Defies Judge, Bans 'Jesus' or 'God Bless You' from Veterans' Funerals," BeliefNet.com, July 1, 2011, http://www.beliefnet.com/columnists/on_the_front_lines_of_the_culture_wars/2011/06/va-cemetery-defies-judge-bans-religious-words-from-services.html; Dave Bohon, "Judge Rules Pastor Can Pray 'in Jesus' Name' at Memorial Day Service," *The New American*, May

28, 2011, http://www.thenewamerican.co m/culture/faith-and-morals/item/928-jud ge-rules-pastor-can-pray-%e2%80%9cin -jesus-name%e2%80%9d-at-memorial -day-service.

7. Ed Whelan, "Seventh Circuit Nominee David Hamilton: 'Allah' Yes, 'Jesus' No," *National Review Online*, March 26, 2009, http://www.nationalreview.com/be nch-memos/50337/seventh-circuit-nomin ee-david-hamilton-allah-yes-jesus-no/ed -whelan.

8. Katherine Driessen and Mike Morris, "Mayor's Decision to Drop Subpoenas Fails to Quell Criticism," *Houston Chronicle*, October 29, 2014, http://www .chron.com/news/politics/houston/article /Mayor-set-to-make-announcement-on-s ermon-subpoenas-5855458.php.

Chapter 9 Now How Much Would You Pay?

1. David Farmer, *The Oxford Dictionary of Saints*, fifth ed., rev. (Oxford: Oxford University Press, 2011), 170; Pedro de Ribadeneyra, *The Lives of the Early Martyrs* (New York: D. & J. Sadler & Co., 1878), 551–62. This story was recorded by a number of early church fathers, including Basil of Caesarea, Ephrem the Syrian, John Chrysostom, and Gregory of Nyssa.

2. Jean Cocteau, "Jean Cocteau Quotes," accessed May 7, 2015, www.poem hunter.com/jean-cocteau/quotations/.

3. As quoted in John R. W. Stott, *The Message of Acts* (Leicester, England: InterVarsity, 1994), 142.

4. "Jim Elliot Quote," Billy Graham Center: Archives, Wheaton College, May 31, 2012, http://www2.wheaton.edu/bgc/ archives/faq/20.htm.

5. Tertullian, "Quotations," accessed May 7, 2015, http://www.tertullian.org/ quotes.htm.

Chapter 10 New and Lasting

1. Christina Ng, "Texas Couple Makes it From Streets to Altar With Church's Help," *ABC News*, April 9, 2013, http://abc news.go.com/US/texas-couple-makes

-streets-altar-churchs/story?id=1890927 0#.UWohDivrlU0.

2. Samuel Hugh Moffett, *A History of Christianity in Asia*, vol. 2: 1500–1900 (Maryknoll, NY: Orbis, 2005), 327–28.

3. Taylor Field, *Upside-Down Leadership: Rethinking Influence and Success* (Birmingham, AL: New Hope, 2012), 13–14.

4. "Saul of Tarsus," *Calvary Crosslink*, January 22, 2012, http://nl.a.youve rsion.com/events/65282.

5. Warren W. Wiersbe, *The Wiersbe Bible Commentary: New Testament* (Colorado Springs: David C. Cook, 2007), 350.

6. Dr. John Sorenson, "Matthew 9:37–38," sermon at Houston's First Baptist Church, July 27, 2014.

Chapter 11 Connecting the Dots

1. Johnny Hunt, "The Formation of Paul's Worldview," sermon on Acts 9:20–25, May 22, 2005, http://www.sermon search.com/sermon-outlines/25109/the -formation-of-pauls worldview/.

2. Ben Stuart, *This Changes Everything: Lessons from James* (Nashville: Lifeway, 2013), 9.

3. "Dwight L. Moody," *Wholesome Words: Echoes from Glory*, accessed April 3, 2015, http://www.wholesomewords. org/echoes/moody.html.

Chapter 12 Prayer vs. Pride

1. A book that was very influential in my life on the subject of fasting was Ronnie Floyd, *The Power of Prayer and Fasting* (Nashville: B&H, 2010).

2. Benjamin Franklin, "The Autobiography of Benjamin Franklin, page 42," *The Electric Ben Franklin*, accessed April 2, 2015, http://www.ushistory.org/franklin /autobiography/page42.htm.

3. C. S. Lewis, "Mere Christianity," *The Complete C. S. Lewis Signature Classics* (New York: HarperOne, 2002), 105.

4. William Ernest Henley, "Invictus," *Poetry Foundation*, http://www.poetry foundation.org/poem/182194. Emphasis added.

Chapter 13 Unstoppable Impact

1. Petronius Arbiter, *The Satyricon*, trans. by W. C. Firebaugh, Project Gutenberg ebook, October 22, 2012, http://www.gutenberg.org/files/5225/5225-h/5225-h.htm.

2. Plato, *Timaeus*, translated by Benjamin Jowett, Project Gutenberg ebook, January 15, 2013, http://www.gutenberg.org/files/1572/1572-h/1572-h.htm.

3. Gallup, "More Than 9 in 10 Americans Continue to Believe in God," Gallup.com, June 3, 2011, http://www.gallup.com/poll/147887/americans-continue-believe-god.aspx.

4. Dr. Walt Baker of Dallas Theological Seminary spoke at the "Breakaway GO! Missions Conference" at Grace Bible Church in the late 1990s and shared these labels of scenery, machinery, and ministry.

Appendix 1: Taking the Next Step in Prayer

1. Houston's First member and friend Mary Ann Bridgwater first showed me this prayer acrostic; www.praytheword.org.

Gregg Matte is the senior pastor of Houston's First Baptist Church. Under his leadership, this historic church founded in 1841 has experienced tremendous growth and has become a multisite church with five campuses.

Before coming to Houston's First in 2004, Gregg founded Breakaway Ministries at Texas A&M University—the largest college Bible study in the nation. What started in his apartment with twelve participants grew to a weekly gathering of more than four thousand students under his leadership. He continues to serve on Breakaway's board of directors.

Gregg holds a bachelor's degree in marketing from Texas A&M and a master's degree from Southwestern Baptist Theological Seminary. Gregg received the Outstanding Alumni Award from the Mays Business School at Texas A&M and was the first pastor to receive that honor in the history of the award.

As well as a pastor, he is the author of *Finding God's Will* and *I AM Changes Who I Am*. Gregg married Kelly in 1997 and together they have a son, Greyson (2001), and a daughter, Valerie (2008).